MEASURING MORTALITY, FERTILITY, AND NATURAL INCREASE:

A Self-Teaching Guide to Elementary Measures

James A. Palmore
and
Robert W. Gardner

The East-West Center, Honolulu 96848
© 1983 by the East-West Center. All rights reserved.
Sixth impression 1991

Library of Congress Cataloging in Publication Data

Palmore, James A.
  Measuring mortality, fertility, and natural increase.

  Combined rev. ed. of: Measuring fertility and natural
increase. 1972 and Measuring mortality.
  "January 1983."
  Bibliography: p.
  Includes index.
  1. Demography. 2. Vital statistics. 3. Mortality—
Statistical methods. 4. Fertility, Human—Statistical
methods. I. Gardner, Robert W. II. Title.
HB849.4.P34   1983   304.6'01'5195   82-24171
ISBN 0-86638-004-3

Contents

Preface   *ix*

Chapter 1: Rates, Ratios, Percentages,
    and Probabilities   *1*

Chapter 2: Mortality   *9*

Chapter 3: Fertility, Natural Increase,
    and Reproduction Rates   *59*

Appendix 1: Notation and Formulas   *121*

Appendix 2: Relationship between
    q_x and M_x Values   *125*

Appendix 3: Answers to Selected
    Exercises   *129*

References   *135*

Tables and Figures

Tables

1. Ratios frequently used in demographic work   *3*

2. Calculation of number of person-years lived during one year in a hypo-
    thetical small town having a population of 700 persons on January 1   *4*

3. Highest and lowest death rates, by region: recent years   *11*

4. Highest and lowest age-specific death rates (ASDRs): recent years   *14*

5. Age-specific and crude death rates for three hypothetical populations   *15*

6. Age-specific death rates (ASDRs) and populations for Maine and South
    Carolina: 1930   *17*

7. Age standardization of crude death rates for the United States (1978)
    and Venezuela (1977)   *22*

8. Formulas for direct age-standardization of the crude death rate for two
    hypothetical populations   *25*

9. Standardized death rates for selected countries and years   *26*

10. Infant mortality rates, by age, for selected countries, by region   *30*

11. Highest and lowest infant mortality rates, by region: latest available
    data   *32*

12. Complete life table for females: United States, 1969–71   *36*

13. Abridged life table for females: United States, 1978   *46*

14. Age composition of the stationary population and the actual population for U.S. white females: 1978   *49*

15. Crude death rates and life table death rates for U.S. white females: selected years, 1900–77   *50*

16. Survivors to exact age x (ℓ_x) of 100,000 male babies (ℓ_0): Sri Lanka and United States, selected years   *54*

17. Examples of high and low values of life expectancy at birth for males and females: recent years   *55*

18. Life expectancies at selected exact ages for U.S. males and females, by color: 1978   *55*

19. Life expectancies for U.S. white males and females at exact ages 0, 40, and 70: 1850–1978   *56*

20. Highest and lowest crude birth rates, by region: recent years   *62*

21. Distribution of countries, by level of crude birth rate: 1974–78   *63*

22. Average crude rates of natural increase, by region: 1970–75   *65*

23. Approximate number of years a population takes to double, triple, and quadruple in size, given specified rates of growth   *66*

24. Estimates of mid-year population, by region: selected years, 1650–1978   *67*

25. Lowest and highest age-specific fertility rates (ASFRs) per 1,000 women: 1970s   *70*

26. Age-specific fertility rates per 1,000 women: Hutterites and all U.S. women, around 1940   *72*

27. Distribution of major countries and territories, by level of age-specific fertility rates   *73*

28. Birth rates by live birth order and percentage change in rates: United States, selected years, 1942–75   *78*

29. Crude birth rates and directly standardized birth rates, for selected countries and dates   *80*

30. Crude birth rates and directly standardized birth rates: United States, selected years, 1940–75   *81*

31. General fertility rates for selected countries, age-standardized by the direct method: recent years   *82*

32. Observed general fertility rates and age-standardized general fertility rates with Sweden (1970), India (1971), and Republic of Korea (1972) as standard populations: India, Sweden, Philippines, Ireland, United States   *84*

33. Calculation of total fertility rates for the United States: 1957, 1967, and 1975   *86*

34. Calculation of the gross reproduction rate for Costa Rica: 1960   *89*

35. Estimated crude birth rates and gross reproduction rates for world regions: around 1970   *91*

36. Distribution of world regions, by level of gross reproduction rate: 1965–75   *92*

37. Calculation of the gross and net reproduction rates and the length of a generation for the United States, 1975   *93*

38. Selected illustrative reproduction measures, comparing intrinsic and crude rates   *96*

39. Gross and net reproduction rates for Europe: depression years, post World War II, and recent past   *98*

40. Gross and net reproduction rates, by color: United States, 1905–77   *99*

41. Percentage ever married and number of children ever born for women of ages 45–49 and 30–34: United States, 1940–78   *105*

42. Number of children ever born per 1,000 women and per 1,000 married women, by age: United States, selected years, 1940–78   *106*

43. Number of children ever born to ever married women, by woman's education and color, for women 35–39 years old in 1970, and percentage of women ever married in each educational category, by color: United States   *107*

44. Number of children ever born to married women living with husbands, by husband's occupation in 1969 and by color, for women 35–39 years old in 1970, and percentage of husbands in each occupational category: United States   *108*

45. Number of children ever born to married women, by family income in 1969 and by presence of wife in labor force, for women 35–39 years old in 1970, and percentage of wives in each income category: United States   *109*

46. Birth probabilities within successive birth intervals 2, 3, and 4–8, by duration of interval and contraceptive use status: Philippines and Republic of Korea   *114*

47. Year in which any birth interval had to begin, given age at beginning of interview, for a survey taking place in 1971: all intervals   *116*

Figures

1. Age-specific male death rates for Madagascar, 1966, and Sweden, 1967   *13*

2. Age-specific fertility rates for China (Taiwan), the United States, and Sweden: 1970–71   *71*

Preface

A simple book on demographic methods had been needed for many years when Ronald Freedman suggested to the first author that he write a series of self-teaching guides about elementary demographic measures. In the fall of 1969, two short manuals were drafted: *Measuring Mortality: A Self-Teaching Guide to Elementary Measures* and *Measuring Fertility and Natural Increase: A Self-Teaching Guide to Elementary Measures.* In 1971 revised drafts were published as Papers of the East-West Population Institute (Nos. 15 and 16). The manuals have since been revised two additional times. The present volume is, hence, the fourth edition. For this edition, we have combined the two manuals into one longer manual because few readers have asked for only one or the other.

We believe the volume may be useful for several kinds of readers. In introductory courses on population issues, usually neither the instructor nor the students want to spend much class time discussing such basic demographic measures as the crude birth rate. The *Guide* is designed to familiarize the graduate, undergraduate, and even advanced high school student with most measures of mortality and fertility that are likely to be encountered in such a course. It may also be used as an introductory text in courses that concentrate on demographic methods. A third use is in social science courses other than population. Most demographic methods are readily modified for other kinds of social science measurement. For example, the instructor of an introductory course in methodology for sociologists might draw on this book for some portion of the course.

The *Guide* is designed for self-teaching. Most instructors will find that they need a maximum of three hours of class time to review the exercises with students and to clarify any points that are confusing. Our classroom experience with these exercises, many of which appeared in the earlier editions of the *Guide,* and comments we have received from other instructors, in Asia as well as the United States, have enabled us to incorporate into this edition changes that should enhance the *Guide*'s self-teaching value.

Each chapter explains elementary principles of demographic measurement, and each has the following parts:

(a) definitions of measures and examples of their usual values;

(b) exercises and questions for the student that emphasize interpretation rather than computation; and

(c) references to other sources that use the measures in interesting or important ways.

For much of the discussion, we borrow heavily from standard references on demographic methods, including:

George W. Barclay, *Techniques of Population Analysis* (New York: John Wiley and Sons, Inc., 1958);

A.J. Jaffe, *Handbook of Statistical Methods for Demographers* (Washington, D.C.: U.S. Bureau of the Census, U.S. Government Printing Office, 1951);

Henry S. Shryock, Jacob S. Siegel, and Associates, *The Methods and Materials of Demography* (Washington, D.C.: U.S. Government Printing Office, 1971), 2 volumes. (A condensed edition of this last work is available in one volume from Academic Press, 1978.)

Another valuable resource has been a manuscript copy of the "Manual of Demographic Research Techniques," by Donald J. Bogue and Evelyn Kitagawa (forthcoming). We have also consulted various manuals of the United Nations. Additional citations are provided at appropriate places in the text, and a complete list of references is found at the end of the *Guide.*

In preparing a volume like this, the authors are always indebted to colleagues and students who have patiently read earlier versions and contributed to the final clarity of the product through their comments. We are particularly indebted to Ronald Freedman, who not only first suggested the idea but also provided several of the exercises used here and made many valuable comments. We have also benefited from comments made by Reynolds Farley, Nathan Keyfitz, Susan Palmore, Monica Fong, David Swanson, Davor Jedlicka, Mead Cain, J.S. MacDonald, Robert Retherford, Peter Smith, Sandra Ward, Robert Hearn, Maureen St. Michel, and Griffith Feeney. The tables for the present edition were updated and revised by Dawn Schenker, Maureen St. Michel, and Florentina Reyes Salvail. We are grateful to the many students at the University of Michigan and the University of Hawaii who discovered errors and tried their best to save us from making simple matters seem complex. Nevertheless, we must bear responsibility for any errors that may remain. We would appreciate it if readers would bring them to our attention.

James A. Palmore
Robert W. Gardner
August 1982

Rates, Ratios, Percentages, and Probabilities 1

It is possible to measure the incidence of an event (for example, death) in many ways. In this chapter, we discuss rates of various types, and we also briefly discuss ratios, percentages, and probabilities, using the measurement of mortality as an illustration.

For any demographic measurement of an event, we want to be precise about:

(a)   what time period is the referent,

(b)   what group of people are referred to, and

(c)   what type of occurrence we are measuring.

Differences in the specificity of each of these three factors are responsible for the existence of many different demographic measures.

Ratios, Proportions, and Percentages

You are probably already familiar with the everyday use of ratios and percentages. Examples of everyday ratios are:

(a)   "I'll give you 2 to 1 that Japan wins the gymnastics medal at the next Olympics" and

(b)   "Miller's Department Store is twice as expensive as Pharoah's."

Generally, a *ratio* is a single number that expresses the relative size of two numbers. The result of dividing a number X by another number Y is the ratio of X to Y, i.e.:

$$\frac{X}{Y} = \text{ratio of } X \text{ to } Y.$$

Many ratios are used in demographic measurement, several of which are defined in Table 1. For any ratio, we should specify carefully what type of event or population is the referent. For example, the sex ratio (males per 100 females) might refer to:

(a)   the total population of the United States in 1981,

(b)   the persons 15–34 years of age in West Malaysia in 1957, or

(c)   the live births occurring in England and Wales in 1975, 1976, and 1977.

We can also use the sex ratio in mortality analysis. For example, we might compare the number of male deaths with the number of female deaths from a certain disease.

Proportions are a special type of ratio in which the denominator includes the numerator. We might, for example, calculate the proportion of all deaths that occurred to males, as in the following formula:

$$\text{Proportion of deaths that occurred to males} = \frac{D^m}{D^m + D^f} = \frac{\text{deaths to males}}{\text{deaths to males plus deaths to females.}}$$

Percentages are a special type of proportion, one in which the ratio is multiplied by a constant, 100, so that the ratio is expressed per 100. If you leaf through the tables in this volume, you will see many examples of ratios, proportions, and percentages. All of these simple measures are useful to the demographer.

Rates

Generally, ratios and percentages are useful for analyzing the composition of a set of events or of a population. Rates, in contrast, are used to study the dynamics of change. A *rate* refers to the occurrence of events over a given interval in time. We can define a rate of incidence in general terms as follows:

$$\text{Rate of incidence} = \frac{\text{number of events that occur within a given time interval}}{\begin{array}{c}\text{number of members of the population} \\ \text{who were exposed to the risk of the} \\ \text{event during the same time interval.}\end{array}}$$

Specifying the number of persons "exposed to risk" in the denominator is important. If you were studying mortality over a one-year period in country *A*, you should note that a person who died before the year ended was not exposed to risk for the whole year and

Table 1. Ratios frequently used in demographic work

Ratio	Formula[a]	Definition
Dependency ratio	$k \left[\dfrac{_{20}P_0 + {_\infty}P_{65}}{_{45}P_{20}} \right]$	$100 \times \dfrac{\text{no. of persons under 20 or over 64}}{\text{no. of persons 20–64 years old}}$
Sex ratio	$k \dfrac{P_i^m}{P_i^f}$	$100 \times \dfrac{\text{no. of males in group } i}{\text{no. of females in group } i}$
Population density	$\dfrac{P_i}{a_i}$	$\dfrac{\text{no. of persons in geographic area } i}{\text{no. of sq. km. (or miles) of land area in geographic area } i}$
Child-woman ratio	$k \left[\dfrac{_5P_0}{_{35}P_{15}^f} \right]$ or $k \left[\dfrac{_5P_0}{_{30}P_{15}^f} \right]$	$1{,}000 \times \dfrac{\text{no. of children under 5 years}}{\text{no. of females 15–49 or 15–44 years old}}$

Note: See Appendix 1 for a discussion of the notation system and formulas used in this volume.

a   The symbol ∞ stands for infinity. In the formulas presented here, it refers to the oldest persons in the population.

neither was a child who was born halfway through the year. People who moved to country *A* only one month before the year ended were not exposed to the risk of dying in country *A* for the whole year either.

The concept of "person-years lived" is the ideal way to specify the population exposed to the risk of an event. It is simply the product of the number of persons multiplied by the number of years, or fractions of years, that each person lived in a given place. Table 2 presents the calculation of person-years lived for a hypothetical small town. Note that the population at either the beginning or the end of the year is a different figure from the number of person-years lived. The example is unusual because:

(a)   no net growth occurred in the town,

(b)   200 people died on one day (January 15), and

Table 2. Calculation of number of person-years lived during one year in a hypothetical small town having a population of 700 persons on January 1

Number of persons	Events and dates		Number of days lived	Number of person-years lived
700	Alive on January 1			
493	Lived in the town continuously from January 1 to December 31		179,945	493.00
1	Born January 11		354	.97
1	Born January 11	Died November 9	302	.83
200		Died January 15	3,000	8.22
1	Born February 21	Died April 27	65	.18
1	Born March 6	Died March 31	25	.07
2		Died April 8	196	.54
94	Born April 10		24,910	68.25
4	Arrived from outside town April 18		1,032	2.83
1		Died June 1	152	.42
1		Died June 5	156	.43
1	Born June 7		207	.57
1		Died June 22	173	.47
1	Born June 24		190	.52
1		Died June 30	181	.50
1		Left town August 16	228	.62
1	Born August 26		127	.35
1	Born September 13	Died November 13	61	.17
1	Born October 1		91	.25
2	Born October 7		170	.46
2	Born October 19		146	.40
100	Arrived from outside town October 25		6,700	18.36
Total person-years lived				598.41
700	Alive on December 31			

Source: Modified from Barclay (1958:39).

(c)   100 people arrived from elsewhere on one day (October 25). Such occurrences would be highly unusual, but they illustrate how the number of person-years lived can be quite different from the population at either the beginning or the end of a period under study.

The calculation of actual person-years lived for a real population of any large size would be difficult, if not impossible. For this reason, most demographic rates are based on an approximation of person-years lived in the denominator. We assume that births, deaths, and movements in and out of the population occur at uniform intervals during the period under study. If that were true, then the number of people alive at the middle of the year (July 1) would equal the number of person-years lived. This population alive at the middle of the year is called the midyear or central population, and so a death (or birth) rate with it as a denominator is known as a central rate.

If (as we have assumed) births, deaths, and movements in and out of the population are evenly distributed throughout the year:

(a)   for every birth at midnight on January 1, there is one at midnight on December 30. The average number of person-years lived for the two births is:

$$[(\frac{364}{365} + \frac{1}{365})/2] = 1/2.$$

(b)   for every death at midnight on January 15, there is one at midnight on December 16. The average number of person-years lived for the two deaths is:

$$[(\frac{15}{365} + \frac{350}{365})/2] = 1/2.$$

This is why the midyear population is usually a good approximation of person-years lived. Note, however, the significance of the assumption of evenly distributed births, deaths, and movements in and out of the population. In a population subject to conditions like the small town of Table 2, the midyear population is not a good approximation of the number of person-years lived.

We can further illustrate the errors that might arise from using the midyear assumption by referring to the infant mortality rate. The infant mortality rate is defined as the number of deaths to children under age one in a given year per thousand children born. In fact, infant deaths are not evenly distributed throughout the first year of life: most infant deaths occur during the first month of life. Suppose that in the last month of 1981 there was a large number of births and that there were fewer births in 1982 than in 1981. During the first months of 1982, there would be many deaths of infants who were born during the preceding year. If we simply related the number of infant deaths in 1982 to the births in 1982, we would exaggerate the infant mortality rate. We will comment on ways of dealing with this problem when we discuss the life table, but here the point is to illustrate that (1) the events being measured and the population at risk must be related properly to each other, and (2) assumptions, though necessary, are not always accurate.

To calculate a midyear population, one would usually take the population on January 1 of year X, add it to the population on January 1 of year $X+1$, then divide by 2. For our small town in Table 2, the midyear population is $[(700 + 700)/2] = 700$.

Exercise 1*

Construct a small hypothetical population, specifying the same characteristics and events as are specified in Table 2. Calculate the midyear population. Calculate the person-years lived. Are they close to the same value? If not, why not?

A Note of Caution

Because demographers come from many academic disciplines and for various historical reasons, the "rates" used by demographers are not always rates as we have described them above. By convention, for example, some ordinary percentage figures are called rates. One illustration of such usage is the "literacy rate," which is simply the percentage of the population that is literate in some specified language. To avoid confusing real and unreal rates is not easy. One must learn how to determine whether a rate that is given is really a rate, a simple percentage, or something else. In each case, the definition of the measure should be clear enough to allow readers to decide whether it is a rate or another type of measure. Most of the rates discussed in this guide are, fortunately, real rates; the exceptions are the survival rates discussed in connection with the life table and the reproduction rates of Chapter 3, which are both more like probabilities than rates.

Probabilities

As we have noted, rates refer to the occurrence of events over a given interval of time. The denominator of a rate is, ideally, the number of person-years of exposure and more commonly the average population

---

* Answers to selected exercises are found in Appendix 3.

exposed to the event in question. A *probability* is similar to a rate, with one important difference: the denominator is composed of all those persons in the given population *at the beginning of the period of observation.* Thus, if ten people die in one year out of a population that numbered 1,000 at the start of the year, we say that the probability of dying for this group during that year was 10/1000, or 0.01000. Note that this is different from the death rate for the same period, which would be (if the deaths were evenly distributed) $10/[1/2(1000+990)] = 10/995 = 0.01005$. For populations experiencing only deaths (and not migration or births), probabilities of dying will always be smaller than the comparable death rates, because the numerators will be the same but the denominators will be larger. We shall deal with the concept of probabilities more when we reach the discussion of the life table and $_nq_x$ in Chapter 2.

With this brief introduction to concepts used in the measurement of any demographic event, we now turn to the measures used in studying mortality.

Mortality

2

We begin with measures of mortality for historical reasons. For most of human history, the fate of a population—whether it grew, stagnated, or failed to survive—depended more on mortality than on fertility or migration. As recently as three decades ago, mortality and its control were the central issue in population policy and demographic interest for most of the world's countries, and it is only more recently that the study of fertility and migration has gained the demographic spotlight. Consequently, much of the earliest work on the development of demographic measures concentrated on measures of mortality. For example, work on the life table (discussed later in this chapter) began as early as the mid seventeenth century. We start with even simpler measures, however, such as the crude death rate.

Crude Death Rate

The *crude death rate* (CDR) is defined as the number of people dying in a given year divided by the number of people in the population in the middle of that year. Conventionally, we express the rate per 1,000 persons. As a formula, we have:

$$\text{CDR} = 1,000 \left[\frac{\text{number of deaths}}{\text{midyear population}} \right] = k \frac{D}{P}$$

where D = deaths in the year,
P = midyear population, and
k = 1,000.

For example, country A had a population of 550 on December 31, 1980, and a population of 650 on December 31, 1981. The mid-1980 population is then: $[(550 + 650)/2] = 600$. If 15 deaths occurred in country A in 1980, the crude death rate would be: $(15/600 \times 1,000 = 25$.

In the 1970s, crude death rates for countries with a population of one million or more ranged from about 4 to about 26 per 1,000 per annum (see Table 3). In other words, for each 1,000 persons exposed to the risk of dying in the 1970s, between 4 and 26 died, depending upon the country.

Exercise 2

The following statements about mortality are all inadequate in some way. Specify the inadequacies:

1. Ten people died in 1981.
2. Ten people died in 1981 out of a population that numbered 1,000 on December 31, 1981.
3. Ten people died out of 1,000 alive on June 30, 1981, in West Countridad.

Age-Specific Death Rates

Of course, the crude death rate is a crude measure. As we all know, an 85-year-old man is more likely to die than a 20-year-old woman. Men fighting on the front lines are more likely to die than those waiting at home. In other words, different subgroups in a population are exposed to different risks of dying—because of their occupation or their age or some other characteristic. Because of these differentials in exposure to the risk of dying, demographers often use *specific death rates.* A specific death rate is one that refers only to some subgroup in the population. The most commonly used specific death rates are *age-specific death rates.*

We may define an age-specific death rate (ASDR) as in the following formula:

$$_nM_x = \text{ASDR for age group } x \text{ to } x+n = 1,000 \times \frac{\text{number of deaths to persons age } x, x+n}{\text{midyear population of persons age } x, x+n} = k\,\frac{_nD_x}{_nP_x}$$

where $_nD_x$ = deaths to persons of age group x to $x+n$,

$_nP_x$ = midyear population of age group x to $x+n$, and

$k = 1,000$.

Table 3. Highest and lowest death rates, by region: recent years

Region and country	Year or period	Crude death rates (per 1,000) High	Low
Africa			
Burundi	1974–75	25.5	
Angola	1974–75	25.3	
Egypt	1978		10.5
South Africa (white population)	1974–75		8.4
America, North			
Haiti	1974–75	17.4	
Honduras	1976	13.7	
Puerto Rico	1977		6.0
Costa Rica	1977		4.3
America, South			
Bolivia	1975	18.0	
Peru	1974–75	13.6	
Brazil	1974–75		8.8
Chile	1976		7.7
Asia (excluding U.S.S.R.)			
Yemen Arab Republic	1974–75	26.3	
Nepal	1974–75	22.5	
Japan	1977		6.0
Hong Kong	1977		5.2
Singapore	1978		5.2
Europe (excluding U.S.S.R.)			
Hungary	1978	13.1	
Austria	1978	12.5	
Spain	1977		7.7
Albania	1974–75		6.9
Oceania			
Papua New Guinea	1974–75	17.5	
New Zealand	1977		8.4
Australia	1978		7.6
U.S.S.R.	1977		9.6

Note: Many of these rates are estimates and vary in reliability. Countries for which data were known to be incomplete or of unknown reliability have been omitted. Countries with populations of less than 1 million are excluded.

Source: United Nations Statistical Office, Department of Economic and Social Affairs, 1978 *Demographic Yearbook* (1979, Table 18).

Figure 1 shows two typical patterns of age-specific death rates, one for an economically developed country, the other for a less developed country. Note that in both cases the death rates are highest for the very young and the very old. Also look at the maximum and minimum figures shown for age-specific death rates in Table 4. Most of the highest age-specific rates are found in Africa. That the highest rates for many ages are for the African nations shown does not necessarily mean that other countries may not have rates as high or higher. Data needed to calculate age-specific rates, however, are simply not available for many high-mortality countries, and we therefore present the range as it appears in reported data from the United Nations *Demographic Yearbook* for 1978. The lowest rates shown are generally for European countries. It is likely that these lower figures are really the lowest, since countries with low death rates usually also have better systems for collecting demographic data on mortality.

The Effect of Age Composition on the Crude Death Rate

The crude death rate is a weighted sum of age-specific death rates. Take the following simple calculations:

Ages	Number of persons in midyear population	Number of deaths in year z	Death rate in year z (per 1,000)
0–34 years	2,000	40	20
35 and over	1,000	80	80
Total, all ages	3,000	120	40

The crude death rate is 40 for this hypothetical population. It is a weighted sum of two age-specific rates: 20 and 80. The weights are the proportion of the total population in each age group in the midyear population. That is:

$$\text{CDR} = [\frac{2,000}{3,000} \times 20] + [\frac{1,000}{3,000} \times 80] = [\frac{2}{3} \times 20] + [\frac{1}{3} \times 80] =$$

$$\frac{40}{3} + \frac{80}{3} = \frac{120}{3} = 40.$$

In a formula, we can express this basic relationship as follows:

**Figure 1. Age-specific male death rates for Madagascar, 1966, and
Sweden, 1967**

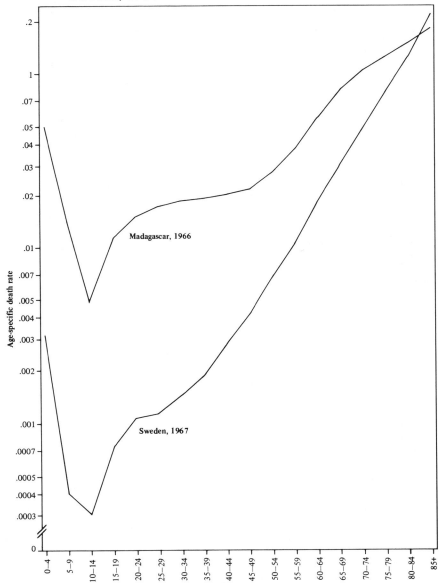

Note: The vertical scale of the graph is logarithmic.

Source: Keyfitz and Flieger (1971:312, 464).

Table 4. Highest and lowest age-specific death rates (ASDRs): recent
         years

| Ages | Highest ASDR | | Lowest ASDR | |
	Rate (per 1,000 population)	Country and year	Rate (per 1,000 population)	Country and year
<1	189.6	Central African Empire (1959–60)	8.1	Sweden (1976)
1–4	45.0	Benin (1961)	0.4	Sweden (1976)
5–9	15.5	Cameroon (1964–65)	0.3	Greece, Austria, Japan, United States (1976)
10–14	8.5	Cameroon (1964–65)	0.2	Japan (1977)
15–19	13.7	Central African Empire (1959–60)	0.4	Hong Kong (1977)
20–24	14.3	Madagascar (1966)	0.7	Netherlands, Hong Kong, Japan (1977)
25–29	16.0	Madagascar (1966)	0.6	Netherlands (1977)
30–34	17.3	Madagascar (1966)	0.8	Netherlands, Norway (1977)
35–39	17.4	Madagascar (1966)	1.2	Switzerland, Netherlands, Israel (1977)
40–44	19.7	Central African Empire (1959–60)	1.7	Greece (1976)
45–49	24.6	Central African Empire (1959–60)	2.9	Greece (1976)
50–54	43.5	Cameroon (1964–65)	4.7	Greece (1976)
55–59	77.1	Cameroon (1964–65)	7.2	Japan (1977)
60–64	58.4	Togo (1961)	12.0	Japan (1977)
65–69	76.5	South Africa (Asiatic population) (1970)	20.4	Japan (1977)
70–74	79.9	Togo (1961)	34.7	Greece (1976)
75–79	86.8	Hungary (1977)	60.4	Norway (1977)
80–84	180.9	Kuwait (1976)	90.4	United States (1976)
85+	307.1	Kuwait (1976)	142.0	Hong Kong (1977)

Note: Many of the rates are estimates that vary in reliability. Countries for which data were
   known to be incomplete or of unknown reliability have been omitted. Countries with
   populations of under 1 million are excluded.

Source: United Nations Statistical Office, Department of Economic and Social Affairs,
   1978 *Demographic Yearbook* (1979, Table 20).

$$CDR = \sum_{x} [_nM_x (\frac{_nP_x}{P})]$$

where $_nP_x$ = midyear population in age group x to $x+n$,

P = total midyear population,

$_nM_x$ = age-specific death rate per 1,000 for age group x to $x+n$, and

$\sum_{x}$ = the sum of the quantity in brackets for all age groups.

The fact that the crude death rate is a function of both the age-specific death rates and the age distribution is demonstrated by the calculations for the three hypothetical populations presented in Table 5. Countries A and B have the same age-specific death rates, but country A's crude death rate is 54 percent higher than country B's. This is a result of country A's having a considerably larger proportion of its population in the youngest age group, which is subject to higher death rates.

Country B and country C have the same crude death rates, but

Table 5. Age-specific and crude death rates for three hypothetical populations

	Country		
Item	A	B	C
Number of persons in midyear population for age group:			
0–4	1,500	500	500
5–39	4,000	5,000	4,000
40+	500	500	1,500
Number of deaths in age group:			
0–4	120	40	50
5–39	40	50	20
40+	40	40	60
Age-specific death rate (per 1,000) for age group:			
0–4	80	80	100
5–39	10	10	5
40+	80	80	40
Crude death rate (per 1,000)	33.3	21.7	21.7

their age-specific death rates are quite different. Country *C* has a much larger proportion of its population in the oldest age group (where we might expect to find a higher death rate) but, in this age group, has an age-specific death rate of only half of that for countries *A* and *B*. Thus, while country *C* has an older population than either country *A* or *B*, its crude death rate is not higher. (This example is designed to demonstrate the relationship between the age distribution and age-specific rates and does not necessarily represent realistic figures for actual countries.)

Two populations may have the same crude death rates even though one has higher death rates than the other in every age group. This would result, for example, if the population with the higher age-specific rates were concentrated in age groups between 5 and 45, so that more of its people were subject to low death rates. It is even possible for one population to have a crude death rate that is lower than another's when the first population has higher death rates at every age. This paradox is illustrated in Table 6, which compares death rates for Maine and South Carolina in 1930, and will be demonstrated again when we discuss standardization. Although Maine has a higher age-specific rate at ages 5–9, South Carolina has higher rates for every other age group. Nevertheless, Maine has a higher crude death rate.

We have illustrated the idea that a crude death rate can be subdivided, or decomposed, into two elements: (1) the age-specific death rates and (2) the age distribution, which determines to what proportion of the population the age-specific rates apply. This decomposition of a crude death rate into rates specific for some set of characteristics and the distribution of the population by that characteristic can be carried out for any characteristic that might help the analysis. For example, it is possible to have sex-specific death rates and the sex distribution. It is also possible to have age-sex-specific death rates (e.g., the death rate for males 20–24 or females 20–24) and the distribution of the population by age and sex. Since mortality rates do vary significantly both by age and by sex, and since data for the population distribution and for deaths are usually available by age and sex, it is common to have such age-sex-specific death rates. In fact, the approach and logic are quite general. There are also death rates specific for age, sex, and occupation simultaneously, although these are less commonly available. Obviously, the characteristics for

Table 6. Age-specific death rates (ASDRs) and populations for Maine and South Carolina: 1930

Ages	Maine			South Carolina		
	ASDR (per 1,000 popula-tion)	Popu-lation	Percent-age dis-tribution of popu-lation	ASDR (per 1,000 popula-tion)	Popu-lation	Percent-age dis-tribution of popu-lation
0–4	20.56	75,037	9.4	23.92	205,076	11.8
5–9	1.86	79,727	10.0	1.85	240,750	13.9
10–14	1.40	74,061	9.3	1.84	222,808	12.8
15–19	2.23	68,683	8.6	4.26	211,345	12.2
20–24	3.70	60,575	7.6	6.45	166,354	9.6
25–34	3.91	105,723	13.3	8.71	219,327	12.6
35–44	5.45	101,192	12.7	12.42	191,349	11.0
45–54	10.85	90,346	11.3	19.94	143,509	8.3
55–64	20.36	72,478	9.1	33.13	80,491	4.6
65–74	52.19	46,614	5.8	61.47	40,441	2.3
75+	136.45	22,396	2.8	141.36	16,723	1.0
All ages		796,832	99.9		1,738,173	100.1
Crude death rate (per 1,000 population)	13.9			12.9		

Note: Deaths and populations of unknown ages excluded. Total percentages do not equal 100.0 because of rounding.

which it is useful to decompose a death rate (or any other rate) are usually those that might make a difference in the death rate. There would be little point in calculating death rates specific for eye color, for example, unless eye color had some bearing on mortality.

First Set of Multiple-Choice Questions

1. In two countries, *A* and *B*, the age-specific death rates per 1,000 are as follows:

Ages	Country *A*	Country *B*
0–4	70	70
5–24	5	5
25–44	10	10
45–64	30	30
65 and over	80	80

Which of the following is true?

(a) The crude death rate is higher in country *A* than in country *B*.

(b) The crude death rate is higher in country *B* than in country *A*.

(c) The crude death rates are equal in the two countries.

(d) The crude death rate in country *A* may be higher, lower, or the same as in country *B*.

2. The crude death rates per 1,000 in countries *A* and *B* are as follows for specific areas of the two countries:

Areas	Country *A*	Country *B*
Metropolitan areas	15	14
Small towns	17	15
Rural areas	30	29

The crude death rate for the whole country is:

(a) definitely less in *A* than in *B*.

(b) definitely less in *B* than in *A*.

(c) probably higher in *A* than in *B*, but the reverse is possible.

(d) probably higher in *B* than in *A*, but the reverse is possible.

Standardization

As we have seen, the age composition of the population has a pronounced effect on the crude death rate. Other aspects of population composition may also have such effects. Examples of other variables that influence death rates are:

(a) urban or rural residence (perhaps because of unequal health care facilities, living standards, infrastructures),

(b) different occupational compositions (miners are more subject to risk than judges or most professional workers),

(c) different income compositions (the wealthy can afford better medical care),

(d) sex (women almost universally have lower death rates than men at most ages), and

(e) marital status (the married usually have lower mortality than the single, widowed, or divorced).

Since we are interested here in measuring mortality rather than age or occupational composition, how do we remove, or control for, the effects of these other variables?

We could simply look at the detailed schedule of age-specific or occupation-specific or age-occupation-specific death rates for two countries and compare them. It is useful, however, to have one single measure (like the crude death rate) that has somehow taken into account the effect of any extraneous variable believed to influence the crude death rate. To obtain this, demographers usually use a technique known as *standardization*. [1]

Look again at the age composition of countries *A* and *B* in Table 5. If they both had the same age composition, it is obvious that their crude death rates would be the same—because they have the same age-specific rates. In standardization, the procedure is to apply the same age composition (or occupation composition or whatever) to different sets of specific rates and observe what the crude rate would then be. The age composition used for the standardization is called the standard population. The rates used are those of the actual populations being studied. Age standardization is used to answer the question: How would the crude death rates of two populations compare if they had exactly the same age distribution (the "standard" we select) but each retained its own distinctive age-specific death rates? In this way, we "hold constant" or "control for" the effect of the age distribution, so that any variations in the total death rates must result from real differences in age-specific mortality rates between the two populations.

This same procedure can be applied to any rate comparison that we can separate into two parts: (1) the effect of the differences in distribution of the characteristic and (2) the effect of differences in the characteristic-specific rates. Thus, we could ask: How would populations *A* and *B* compare on the death rate if they had the same (standard) distribution by age and marital status but each retained its own age and marital status-specific death rates?

The standardization technique also applies to many fields outside of demography and to measures other than rates—such as ratios or percentages. In a study comparing the percentage of people voting for a certain political party in cities *A* and *B*, we might ask whether the difference results from differences between the two cities in the distribution of people by age and income status. We could apply the age and income-specific percentages voting for the party in each city

---

1 We discuss only the technique of direct standardization in this *Guide*. For a discussion of indirect standardization, see Barclay (1958: pp. 164–66).

to a standard age and income distribution to ascertain whether the difference between cities still persists or is modified.

For illustrative purposes, we again take a simple example. Two countries, A and B, have the following age-specific death rates and age composition:

| Ages | Country A | | Country B | |
	Midyear population	Death rate per 1,000	Midyear population	Death rate per 1,000
0–44	1,000	25	4,000	30
45 and over	4,000	40	1,000	45

The crude death rates are 37 per 1,000 for country A and 33 per 1,000 for country B. Suppose both countries had the age composition of country A. Then the crude death rates would be 37 for country A and 42 for country B. In this case, we would say that country A was the "standard population" and that 42 was the "standardized crude death rate" for country B. We can also standardize the crude death rates using country B as the standard population. In this case, the standardized rates are 28 for country A and 33 for country B. The following table summarizes the calculations:

Rate	Country A	Country B
Unstandardized crude death rate per 1,000	37	33
Standardized crude death rate per 1,000		
with country A as standard	37	42
with country B as standard	28	33

Note that country A has a higher crude death rate than country B. When we standardize on the age distribution of either country A or country B, however, country B has a higher death rate because the age-specific death rates for country B are higher than those for country A in every age group.

As an example using actual data, we present the calculations for an age standardization of crude death rates for Venezuela in 1977 and the United States in 1978 (Table 7). The crude death rates are 5.65 per 1,000 for Venezuela and 9.11 per 1,000 for the United States. Standardized on the age distribution of Venezuela, the United States death rate would be only 3.74. Standardized on the age distribution of the United States, the Venezuelan death rate would be 11.29. Hence, although the unstandardized crude death rates for the two countries show that the United States has the higher crude death rate, the standardized rates (with either country as standard population) show that Venezuela has higher death rates. The age composition of Venezuela in 1977 was markedly different from that of the United States, Venezuela having a much younger population.

Death rates at different ages tend to be highly correlated. Country *A*, with low death rates at one age, is likely to have relatively low death rates at all other ages. Country *B*, with high death rates at one age, will usually also have high death rates at all ages. When this is true, it means that any standard population selected will produce the same results—the standardized rate for country *B* will exceed the standardized rate for country *A*. The reason is that we are multiplying the same set of numbers (the standard) by higher numbers for country *B* than for country *A* for every age. Ordinarily, standardization under these circumstances will result at least in clarifying the *direction* of the difference. It will show that country *B* has higher mortality than country *A*. Of course, the choice of the standard population, even in this normal case, could affect the *amount* of the mortality difference between countries *A* and *B*. Suppose the mortality difference between countries *A* and *B* is especially large for ages 40—49. Then the amount of the difference in the standardized rates will depend on the proportion of the standard population that is in the age group 40—49.

Sometimes the situation is not so simple. It may be that population *A* has higher death rates than population *B* at some ages but not at others. In this case, not only the *amount* of the difference but also the *direction* after standardization will depend on the standard age distribution selected. In situations like this, the process of standardization depends on the arbitrary choice of a standard and the results are probably misleading and not very worthwhile. Here is a simple example:

Ages	Country *A*		Country *B*	
	Midyear population	Death rate per 1,000	Midyear population	Death rate per 1,000
0—44	1,000	35	4,000	25
45 and over	4,000	50	1,000	75

The crude death rates and the standardized rates are summarized in the following table:

Table 7. Age standardization of crude death rates for the United States (1978) and Venezuela (1977)

Ages	Age-specific death rate (per 1,000)		Age distributions (per 1,000)		Venezuelan deaths with own age distribution (for population of 1,000) (5) (1) × (3)	Venezuelan deaths with U.S. age distribution (for population of 1,000) (6) (1) × (4)	U.S. deaths with own age distribution (for population of 1,000) (7) (2) × (4)	U.S. deaths with Venezuelan age distribution (for population of 1,000) (8) (2) × (3)
	Vene-zuela[a] (1)	U.S.[b] (2)	Vene-zuela[a] (3)	U.S.[c] (4)				
<1	40.3[d]	14.0[b]	34	15	1.37	.60	.21	.48
1–4	2.9[d]	0.5	127	56	.37	.16	.03	.06
5–9	0.7	0.3	136	77	.10	.05	.02	.04
10–14	0.6	0.3	129	85	.08	.05	.03	.04
15–19	1.2	1.0	116	96	.14	.12	.10	.12
20–24	1.8	1.3	97	93	.17	.17	.12	.13
25–29	2.0	1.3	77	82	.15	.16	.11	.10
30–34	2.3	1.4	56	73	.13	.17	.10	.08
35–39	3.1	1.9	46	60	.14	.19	.11	.09
40–44	3.9	3.0	42	52	.16	.20	.16	.13
45–49	5.6	4.7	37	52	.21	.29	.24	.17
50–54	8.5	7.5	29	54	.25	.46	.41	.22
55–59	9.3	11.2	23	52	.21	.49	.58	.26
60–64	21.0	17.8	17	43	.36	.90	.77	.30
65–69	30.1	24.7	14	39	.42	1.17	.96	.35

70–74	46.6	38.1	8	29	.37	1.35	1.10	.30
75+	113.3	96.6[e]	9	42	1.02	4.76	4.06	.87
All ages			1,000	1,000	5.65[f]	11.29[g]	9.11[h]	3.74[i]

a Source: United Nations Statistical Office, Department of Economic and Social Affairs, 1978 *Demographic Yearbook* (1979, Tables 7, 19).

b Calculated by using life table probability of dying for United States, 1978. Source: U.S. National Center for Health Statistics (1980a, Table 5-1).

c Source: U.S. Bureau of the Census (1980, Table 2).

d Estimated on basis of recorded age-specific deaths and estimated age distribution.

e Life table death rate for ages 75+.

f Total is Venezuelan crude death rate.

g Total is Venezuelan death rate standardized on U.S. age distribution.

h Total is U.S. crude death rate.

i Total is U.S. death rate standardized on the Venezuelan age distribution.

Rate	Country A	Country B
Unstandardized crude death rate per 1,000	47	35
Standardized crude death rate per 1,000		
with country A as standard	47	65
with country B as standard	38	35

Note that country A has a higher crude death rate than country B and also has a higher standardized death rate if we standardize on country B's age distribution. If we standardize on country A's age distribution, however, country B has a higher standardized rate. The choice of the standard population has an important effect on the results. In cases like this, techniques other than standardization are often used to summarize the underlying mortality situation. We will shortly examine life table functions that might be used.

Fortunately, cases like the one just presented are somewhat unusual. For this reason, and because standardization is a relatively easy technique to use, it has found widespread use in demographic analyses. The formulas for the age standardization of death rates are given in Table 8. A comparison of the formulas for Populations A and B in the last two rows of the table shows what standardization does—namely, it uses the age composition of the standard population as the weights in obtaining the weighted sum of age-specific rates that cumulate to form the standardized crude death rate.

Many of the developing countries had low crude death rates in the 1960s (see Table 9). Their populations were very young—that is, they had large proportions of people in young age groups—as a result of their histories of high birth rates. For most of the developing countries, age standardization using the age composition of England and Wales in 1961 or the United States in 1960 shows that the developing countries would have much higher crude death rates if they had the age composition of the two more developed nations. For example, Singapore had a crude death rate of 5.9 in 1962. Standardized on the age composition of either the United States or England and Wales, the rate would be above 15. Similar results are evident from standardizing the rates for Barbados in 1965, Costa Rica in 1960, and South Africa in 1961. The reader may find it instructive to make other comparisons in Table 9 to get some intuitive feeling for the effects of age standardization on the crude death rates of the countries listed there. Note that the *amount* of the differences in rates is affected by

Table 8. Formulas for direct age-standardization of the crude death rate for two hypothetical populations

Item	Formula for:	
	Population A	Population B
Number of people in age group $x, x+n$	$_nP_x^A$	$_nP_x^B$
Total population	$P^A = \sum_x {}_nP_x^A$	$P^B = \sum_x {}_nP_x^B$
Deaths in age group $x, x+n$	$_nD_x^A$	$_nD_x^B$
Deaths in total population	$D^A = \sum_x {}_nD_x^A$	$D^B = \sum_x {}_nD_x^B$
Death rate in age group $x, x+n$	$_nM_x^A = \dfrac{_nD_x^A}{_nP_x^A}$	$_nM_x^B = \dfrac{_nD_x^B}{_nP_x^B}$
Crude death rate	$\dfrac{D^A}{P^A} = \dfrac{\sum_x {}_nD_x^A}{\sum_x {}_nP_x^A}$	$\dfrac{D^B}{P^B} = \dfrac{\sum_x {}_nD_x^B}{\sum_x {}_nP_x^B}$
Death rate standardized on age distribution of Population A	$\dfrac{\sum_x (_nP_x^A)(_nM_x^A)}{\sum_x {}_nP_x^A}$	$\dfrac{\sum_x (_nP_x^A)(_nM_x^B)}{\sum_x {}_nP_x^A}$
Death rate standardized on age distribution of Population B	$\dfrac{\sum_x (_nP_x^B)(_nM_x^A)}{\sum_x {}_nP_x^B}$	$\dfrac{\sum_x (_nP_x^B)(_nM_x^B)}{\sum_x {}_nP_x^B}$

the standard population used. To take one example, there is a difference of 4.1 points between the crude death rates of Venezuela and British Guiana. Standardized on the England and Wales composition, the difference is 8.7 points. Standardized on the United States composition and the Mexico composition, the differences are 7.1 and 3.8 respectively.

Table 9. Standardized death rates for selected countries and years

| Country and year | Crude death rate | Standardized death rate using as standard: | | |
		England and Wales, 1961	United States, 1960	Mexico, 1961
Barbados, 1965	7.8	12.1	10.2	5.7
British Guiana, 1956	11.2	21.5	18.1	10.8
South Africa, 1961 (white population)	8.6	12.9	10.5	5.6
Costa Rica, 1960	8.6	17.8	14.8	8.6
Costa Rica, 1966	7.4	12.0	10.4	7.0
United States, 1919–21	12.5	19.4	16.9	11.9
United States, 1967	9.4	11.1	9.1	4.9
Jamaica, 1956	9.4	17.6	15.0	8.9
Jamaica, 1963	8.9	13.7	11.7	7.4
Venezuela, 1965	7.1	12.8	11.0	7.0
Colombia, 1965	9.9	14.9	13.3	9.8
Israel, 1960 (Jewish population)	5.5	10.2	8.3	4.5
Israel, 1967 (Jewish population)	6.6	10.6	8.5	4.4
Singapore, 1962	5.9	19.5	15.7	7.6
Singapore, 1966–68	5.4	16.5	13.4	6.7
France,[a] 1851	22.3	28.4	27.1	24.1
France, 1967	10.9	10.7	8.8	4.5
Sweden, 1778–82	25.9	30.2	29.0	25.6
Sweden, 1828–32	25.8	33.9	30.9	24.4
Sweden, 1943–47	10.7	12.3	10.1	5.7
Sweden, 1967	10.1	9.3	7.4	3.6
England and Wales, 1861	21.6	27.0	25.4	21.5
England and Wales, 1967	11.2	10.8	8.8	4.4

a   Excluding Nice and La Savoie.

Sources: Keyfitz and Flieger (1968, 1971).

Second Set of Multiple-Choice Questions

1. In countries A and B, the age-specific death rates per 1,000 are as follows:

Ages	Country A	Country B
0–4 years	40	29
5–24	20	19
25–54	25	22
55 years and over	60	58

If the crude death rates for the two countries are standardized on the same age distribution, which of the following would be true?
   (a) The standardized death rate is higher in country A than in country B.
   (b) The standardized death rate is higher in country B than in country A.
   (c) The standardized death rates in the two countries are equal.
   (d) The standardized death rates in country A may be higher, lower, or equal to those of country B.

2. The range of values for national crude death rates in the world today is about:
   (a) 10 to 80.
   (b) 5 to 30.
   (c) 10 to 120.
   (d) 2 to 150.

3. Death rates are standardized:
   (a) to eliminate the differential influence of one or more variables.
   (b) to obtain an estimate of the ideal rates.
   (c) to determine the future rates that may be expected.
   (d) to obtain a correct statement of the actual or experienced rates.
   (e) to correct for underregistration of the phenomenon in question.

4. A high sex ratio:
   (a) is immoral.
   (b) indicates a high proportion of males in the population.
   (c) indicates a low proportion of males in the population.
   (d) indicates a high proportion of infants in the population.
   (e) measures the extent of mortality to males in the population.

Exercise 3

In 1968, city A had a crude death rate of 15 per 1,000 and city B a crude death rate of 9. In the same year, the crude death rate of the United States was about 9.

The age-specific death rates of the two cities are standardized on the age distribution of the United States as a whole in 1968. Consider each of the following six possible results and indicate what interpretation you would give them *in the absence of any other information:*

Results	Death rates per 1,000 standardized on the age distribution of the United States	
	City A	City B
Crude death rate	15	9
Case 1	15	9
Case 2	15	15
Case 3	9	9
Case 4	9	15
Case 5	12	10
Case 6	7	10

Exercise 4

You are given the following data for countries A and B:

Areas	Country A		Country B	
	Midyear population	Death rate per 1,000	Midyear population	Death rate per 1,000
Metropolitan areas	500	20	6,000	25
Small towns	1,500	35	1,500	40
Rural areas	8,000	40	2,500	45

Calculate the crude death rates for each country. Also calculate the area-standardized death rates, using (1) country A as the standard population and (2) country B as the standard population. Compare the answers and interpret them.

The Infant Mortality Rate

It is usually difficult to estimate the number of person-years lived for children under age one because the requisite statistics are not collected or not published. Furthermore, for all the reasons stated above, the midyear population is usually a poor estimate of the person-years lived in the age group under one. Hence, demographers use a special method for calculating the death rate for children under one year of age. They call children under age one "infants" and calculate the *infant mortality rate*[2] (IMR) according to the following formula:

$$IMR = k \frac{D_0^z}{B^z}$$

where D_0^z = number of deaths to children under 1 year of age in year z,

B^z = number of live births in year z, and

k = 1,000.

The infant mortality rate is thus closer to being a probability than a rate, since the denominator is persons (infants) exposed to death beginning at a certain time (birth), rather than the number of person-years lived by infants.[3]

As we mentioned earlier, there is a special pattern of mortality during the first years of life. This is illustrated by the data for selected countries and years in Table 10. Deaths are not evenly distributed through the first year of life; instead, a high proportion of infant mortality occurs in the first month of life. Of the deaths in the first month of life, a high proportion occurs during the first week of life, and, of these deaths during the first week of life, a high proportion occurs during the first day. Mortality of children under 28 days of age is generally almost as high or even higher than mortality in the next five months combined; mortality rates for the second half of the first year are always less than half and usually less than one-third of those for the first six months.

In general, the lower the infant mortality rate is, the higher the proportion of deaths that occur in the first month, the first week, and even the first hour of life. This is because the causes of very early infant deaths tend to be congenital malformation, injuries at

---

2 Barclay (1958) calls this rate the "infant death rate" in order to distinguish it from another type of rate for infants used in constructing life tables. (See Barclay [1958: pp. 47 ff., pp. 106 ff., and pp. 138 ff.].) We prefer the present usage, however, to maintain consistency with tables in the United Nations *Demographic Yearbook* and other common reference materials.

3 Demographers often use the IMR in the construction of life tables as the value for $_1q_0$, the probability of dying between birth and the first birthday. (See section on the life table.)

Table 10. Infant mortality rates, by age, for selected countries, by region

Region, country, and year	<1 day old	1 through 6 days old	7 through 28 days old	28 days through 1 year old	All ages under 1 year
Africa					
Liberia, 1970	——— 48.5 (35.3) ———		35.8 (26.1)	53.1 (38.7)	137.3 (100.1)
South Africa, 1971 (white population)	5.0 (23.9)	7.9 (37.8)	1.9 (9.1)	6.1 (29.2)	20.9 (100.0)
Americas					
Guatemala, 1977	——— 8.4 (12.0) ———		9.7 (13.9)	51.7 (74.1)	69.8 (100.0)
Chile, 1974	8.5 (13.0)	9.4 (14.4)	8.2 (12.6)	39.1 (60.0)	65.2 (100.0)
Canada, 1975	5.7 (41.6)	2.4 (17.5)	1.2 (8.8)	4.4 (32.1)	13.7a (100.0)
Asia					
Pakistan, 1968	2.3 (1.9)	36.3 (29.2)	24.7 (19.9)	61.1 (49.2)	124.3 (100.2)
Japan, 1978	2.0 (23.8)	2.5 (29.8)	1.1 (13.1)	2.8 (33.3)	8.4 (100.0)
Europe					
Portugal, 1975	7.9 (20.3)	8.4 (21.6)	5.8 (14.9)	16.9 (43.4)	38.9 (100.2)
Netherlands, 1978	2.4 (25.0)	3.0 (31.3)	1.2 (12.5)	3.0 (31.3)	9.6 (100.1)
Oceania					
Australia, 1977	5.1 (40.8)	2.3 (18.4)	1.3 (10.4)	3.8 (30.4)	12.5 (100.0)

Notes: Rates are the number of deaths of infants per 1,000 live births. Figures in parentheses are percentages of total. Rates are shown only for countries having at least 1,000 infant deaths in given year and populations of 1 million or more. Data from registers that are incomplete or of unknown completeness are not included. The rates for different ages use the same denominator (1,000 live births) as the total. Consequently, the sum of the rates for the different ages equals the total infant mortality rate shown in last column. Totals may not correspond to sum of constituent rates and percentages because of rounding.

a Excludes 0.6 of unknown age.

Source: United Nations Statistical Office, Department of Economic and Social Affairs, 1979 *Demographic Yearbook* (1981. Table 16).

birth, prematurity, and other causes that are not easily prevented by modern medical and health measures. Causes of later infant deaths (such as infectious diseases or poor nutrition) are more susceptible to prevention or treatment. Hence, with the advance of medicine and public health, late infant deaths diminish faster than early deaths, and there is a higher proportion of all infant deaths that are early deaths.

Three additional problems in measuring infant mortality are caused by the following facts: (a) there are seasonal fluctuations in births; (b) many babies are born and die in the same calendar year and are omitted in a count of the population under age one at both the beginning and the end of the year; and (c) in most censuses and surveys, there tends to be a much greater underenumeration of infants than of others, apparently because many parents do not think of infants as persons when asked: "How many persons live here?"

Infant mortality rates during the 1970s ranged from 8.3 to 142.1 (see Table 11). IMRs used to be much higher. Rates as high as 200 have been recorded for Belgium in 1900, France in the period 1851 to 1903, and Sweden in the period 1778 to 1832 (Keyfitz and Flieger, 1968: pp. 24–39). This means, roughly, that for every five infants born in Belgium, France, or Sweden during those years, one died before its first birthday. The infant mortality rate calculated in the simple way described above is sufficiently reliable only when the number of births does not change rapidly from one calendar year to the next. When rapid changes in the number of births occur, adjusted rates of various kinds are needed and can be calculated, but we will leave a discussion of these until later (Appendix 2).

First Set of True-False Questions

Determine whether each of the following statements is true or false:

1. Infant mortality rates are generally higher in the developing countries than they are in the developed countries.
2. According to available data, crude death rates in the developing countries are always higher than those in the developed countries.
3. The developed countries probably never had infant mortality rates as high as those now recorded in many developing countries.
4. The midyear population is always a good estimate of the person-years lived in a given year.

5. On the average, age-specific death rates are high only for persons over age 65.

Table 11. Highest and lowest infant mortality rates, by region: latest available data

Region and country	Year	Infant mortality rate (per 1,000 live births)	
		High	Low
Africa			
Malawi	1972	142.1	
Tunisia	1971	110.9	
Egypt	1975		89.2[a]
South Africa (white population)	1974		18.4
Americas			
Guatemala	1978	69.2	
Chile	1976	59.6	
United States	1977		14.0
Canada	1977		12.4
Asia			
Pakistan	1968	124.3	
Sri Lanka	1977	42.4	
Hong Kong	1978		11.8
Japan	1978		8.4
Europe			
Portugal	1975	38.9	
Yugoslavia	1977	35.6	
Switzerland	1978		8.6
Sweden	1976		8.3
Oceania			
Australia[b]	1977	——— 12.5 ———	
U.S.S.R.	1970–74	——— 25.2 ———	

Note: Rates are shown only for countries having at least 1,000 infant deaths in given year and populations of 1 million or more. Data from registers that are incomplete or of unknown completeness are not included.

a   Provisional rate.

b   Only country in the region eligible for inclusion in table.

Sources: Office of Population Research (1980b:604); United Nations Statistical Office, Department of Economic and Social Affairs, 1978, 1979 *Demographic Yearbooks* (1979, 1980: Table 15).

The Life Table

Rates and ratios provide us with a useful set of measures for answering questions about mortality. There are still many questions, however, that we cannot answer with these measures alone. To cite a few examples:

(1) Out of 100 persons in country A who were 20 years old in 1968, how many are likely to live to age 50?

(2) Immediately after birth in 1950, how many years could a child in country B expect to live?

(3) Among young men and women entering the labor force at ages 20–24, what proportion can be expected to be alive at age 65 (when they are entitled to collect social security benefits)? Of those who do begin to collect benefits at age 65, how many can be expected to survive for one year, two years, three years, etc.?

(4) Is there a measure that can be used to compare the mortality of many countries so that differences in their age distributions will not be distorting factors and so that an arbitrary choice of a standard population for an age standardization will not be necessary?

Questions of this type have immense practical importance. For example, projections of the future population needed to determine the number of schools or hospitals required depend on estimates of how long people survive. In addition, life insurance companies need accurate answers to questions about average life expectancy, for without them they would not be able to construct actuarial tables, on which they base the premiums customers must pay. Such questions as these can best be answered by *life tables,* although the answers are still approximate.

Constructing a life table can be a complex process. Here, we emphasize interpretation rather than computation, beginning with a description of the life table and afterward discussing elementary applications in demographic analysis.

Instead of the more usual notion of a population, suppose we were to consider a population to consist of everyone born in country A during, say, 1879. Demographers would call this group the "1879 birth cohort" for country A. Now suppose we had the death rates for the 1879 birth cohort as it passed through each age, until all members of the cohort had died (presumably almost all would have died by now). In this situation we could answer questions about the survival of members of the cohort from one age to the next, since we would know their entire mortality history. From data of this type, we could construct what is known as a *longitudinal* or *generation* life table, which refers to one birth cohort as it ages. A generation life table can be constructed only after all or almost all the members of the birth cohort have died. Its practical utility is therefore limited. For this reason, and because the required data are not often available, generation life tables are not commonly used.

Let us return to our more usual notion of a population. Suppose we have a set of age-specific death rates that represent the incidence of mortality in each age group for a cross-section of the population over a short period of time (a year, for example). We assume that the age-specific mortality experiences during that time represent the death experience of a whole generation of persons. That is, we assume the death rate of persons 10−14 years old now to be the same death rate that persons 5−9 years old today will have in five years when they become 10−14 years old. Making this assumption, we can determine what the number of survivors at any given age out of an initial group of births would be, according to the given mortality schedule. The life table, then, becomes a model of what would happen to a hypothetical birth cohort *if the age-specific death rates for a given period were to remain constant and were to apply throughout the experience of an entire generation.* Mortality analyses based on life tables are normally based on the assumption that a single mortality schedule applies to a hypothetical group of persons until all the persons have died.

This more common type of life table is called a *period, cross-sectional, current,* or *time-specific* life table. It answers the question: What would be the mortality history and average life expectancy of a cohort of people subject throughout their life history to the age-specific death rates of a particular year or period? The period life table is a mathematical model of the life history of a hypothetical cohort. It is a model because we must make simplifying assumptions in order to construct the table and because it refers to a hypothetical rather than a real birth cohort.

The life table begins with the birth, during one year, of a hypothetical cohort of persons. Usually, the number of births is set arbitrarily at 100,000. This starting number of births is called the "radix" of the life table. The life table record continues until all the members of the cohort have died, deaths at each age occurring in accordance with a mortality schedule that is fixed in advance and does not change. No factors other than mortality operate to reduce the size of the starting cohort; i.e., the hypothetical cohort is "closed" to migration of any kind. At each age, except for the first few years of life, the deaths are assumed to be evenly distributed throughout the year. Hence, half of the deaths to persons between the ages 15 and 16, say, would occur by the time the average person in the cohort has reached the age 15½. Most life tables refer to only one sex, primarily because the death rates for males and females differ substantially.

The conventional life table consists of seven columns, six of which present what are called the "life table functions." A brief description of each column follows. To illustrate, we use a life table for females in the United States in the period 1969–71 (Table 12).

Column 1: Exact Age (x)

Each of the life table functions refers to a specific age or age interval. The first column of the life table specifies the age to which the later columns of the table refer. In the life table, the word "age" is used very precisely, and the precision is emphasized by the addition of the modifier "exact." When we say that a person is exact age 0, we mean that he was just born. When he is exact age 5, he has lived exactly five full years. (In contrast, to say that someone "is 5 years old" means that the person is between exact age 5 and exact age 6—i.e., age 5 on the last birthday.)

The letter x is used to represent exact age. Some of the life table functions refer to the exact age x and some refer to the age interval between exact age x and exact age $x + 1$.

Column 2: Probability of Dying Between Age x and Age x + 1 (q_x)

The second column of the life table (q_x) represents the probability of dying between exact age x and exact age $x + 1$. This column summarizes the life table mortality rates, which are probabilities and thus different from the age-specific death rates discussed earlier in this chapter. The q_x function is the numerical answer to the question: Among persons who reach exact age x, what proportion will die before their next birthday—that is, within one year? The q_x values

Table 12. Complete life table for females: United States, 1969–71

Exact age in years	Probability of dying between age x and age x + 1	Number of survivors at exact age x	Number of deaths between age x and age x + 1	Number of years lived between age x and age x + 1	Total number of years lived after exact age x	Expectation of life (average number of years lived) after exact age x
x	q_x	ℓ_x	d_x	L_x	T_x	e_x
(1)	(2)	(3)	(4)	(5)	(6)	(7)
0	.01746	100,000	1,746	98,511	7,464,410	74.64
1	.00116	98,254	115	98,196	7,365,899	74.97
2	.00077	98,139	75	98,102	7,267,703	74.05
3	.00060	98,064	59	98,034	7,169,601	73.11
4	.00051	98,005	50	97,981	7,071,567	72.16
5	.00043	97,955	42	97,934	6,973,586	71.19
6	.00038	97,913	37	97,894	6,875,652	70.22
7	.00034	97,876	34	97,859	6,777,758	69.25
8	.00031	97,842	30	97,827	6,679,899	68.27
9	.00028	97,812	28	97,798	6,582,072	67.29
10	.00026	97,784	25	97,772	6,484,274	66.31
11	.00025	97,759	25	97,746	6,386,502	65.33
12	.00027	97,734	27	97,721	6,288,756	64.35
13	.00033	97,707	31	97,692	6,191,035	63.36
14	.00040	97,676	40	97,656	6,093,343	62.38
15	.00049	97,636	48	97,612	5,995,687	61.41
16	.00058	97,588	57	97,560	5,898,075	60.44
17	.00066	97,531	64	97,499	5,800,515	59.47
18	.00069	97,467	67	97,434	5,703,016	58.51
19	.00071	97,400	69	97,365	5,605,582	57.55

20	.00072	97,331	70	97,296	5,508,217	56.59
21	.00073	97,261	71	97,225	5,410,921	55.63
22	.00075	97,190	73	97,153	5,313,696	54.67
23	.00077	97,117	75	97,080	5,216,543	53.71
24	.00079	97,042	76	97,004	5,119,463	52.75
25	.00081	96,966	78	96,927	5,022,459	51.80
26	.00083	96,888	81	96,847	4,925,532	50.84
27	.00086	96,807	83	96,766	4,828,685	49.88
28	.00090	96,724	88	96,680	4,731,919	48.92
29	.00096	96,636	92	96,590	4,635,239	47.97
30	.00102	96,544	99	96,495	4,538,649	47.01
31	.00110	96,445	106	96,392	4,442,154	46.06
32	.00119	96,339	115	96,282	4,345,762	45.11
33	.00129	96,224	123	96,162	4,249,480	44.16
34	.00140	96,101	135	96,034	4,153,318	43.22
35	.00152	95,966	145	95,893	4,057,284	42.28
36	.00165	95,821	159	95,742	3,961,391	41.34
37	.00180	95,662	172	95,576	3,865,649	40.41
38	.00197	95,490	188	95,396	3,770,073	39.48
39	.00215	95,302	205	95,199	3,674,677	38.56
40	.00233	95,097	221	94,986	3,579,478	37.64
41	.00251	94,876	239	94,757	3,484,492	36.73
42	.00273	94,637	258	94,508	3,389,735	35.82
43	.00297	94,379	281	94,238	3,295,227	34.91
44	.00325	94,098	305	93,946	3,200,989	34.02

Table 12. (continued)

Exact age in years	Probability of dying between age x and age x + 1	Number of survivors at exact age x	Number of deaths between age x and age x + 1	Number of years lived between age x and age x + 1	Total number of years lived after exact age x	Expectation of life (average number of years lived) after exact age x
x	q_x	ℓ_x	d_x	L_x	T_x	e_x
(1)	(2)	(3)	(4)	(5)	(6)	(7)
45	.00354	93,793	332	93,627	3,107,043	33.13
46	.00384	93,461	360	93,281	3,013,416	32.24
47	.00416	93,101	387	92,908	2,920,135	31.37
48	.00449	92,714	415	92,506	2,827,227	30.49
49	.00484	92,299	447	92,076	2,734,721	29.63
50	.00523	91,852	480	91,611	2,642,645	28.77
51	.00565	91,372	517	91,114	2,551,034	27.92
52	.00611	90,855	555	90,578	2,459,920	27.08
53	.00660	90,300	596	90,002	2,369,342	26.24
54	.00712	89,704	638	89,385	2,279,340	25.41
55	.00768	89,066	684	88,724	2,189,955	24.59
56	.00829	88,382	733	88,015	2,101,231	23.77
57	.00894	87,649	784	87,257	2,013,216	22.97
58	.00962	86,865	835	86,448	1,925,959	22.17
59	.01035	86,030	891	85,584	1,839,511	21.38
60	.01113	85,139	948	84,666	1,753,927	20.60
61	.01200	84,191	1,010	83,686	1,669,261	19.83
62	.01298	83,181	1,080	82,641	1,585,575	19.06
63	.01411	82,101	1,158	81,522	1,502,934	18.31
64	.01538	80,943	1,245	80,320	1,421,412	17.56

Age						
65	.01678	79,698	1,337	79,030	1,341,092	16.83
66	.01832	78,361	1,435	77,643	1,262,062	16.11
67	.02004	76,926	1,542	76,155	1,184,419	15.40
68	.02195	75,384	1,654	74,557	1,108,264	14.70
69	.02407	73,730	1,775	72,842	1,033,707	14.02
70	.02632	71,955	1,894	71,008	960,865	13.35
71	.02879	70,061	2,017	69,053	889,857	12.70
72	.03165	68,044	2,154	66,967	820,804	12.06
73	.03503	65,890	2,308	64,736	753,837	11.44
74	.03893	63,582	2,475	62,345	689,101	10.84
75	.04325	61,107	2,643	59,786	626,756	10.26
76	.04790	58,464	2,800	57,064	566,970	9.70
77	.05295	55,664	2,947	54,191	509,906	9.16
78	.05840	52,717	3,079	51,178	455,715	8.64
79	.06432	49,638	3,193	48,041	404,537	8.15
80	.07097	46,445	3,296	44,798	356,496	7.68
81	.07834	43,149	3,380	41,459	311,698	7.22
82	.08612	39,769	3,425	38,056	270,239	6.80
83	.09419	36,344	3,423	34,632	232,183	6.39
84	.10275	32,921	3,383	31,230	197,551	6.00
85	.11282	29,538	3,332	27,872	166,321	5.63
86	.12462	26,206	3,266	24,573	138,449	5.28
87	.13685	22,940	3,139	21,370	113,876	4.96
88	.14859	19,801	2,943	18,330	92,506	4.67
89	.16006	16,858	2,698	15,509	74,176	4.40

Table 12. (*continued*)

x	q_x	ℓ_x	d_x	L_x	T_x	e_x
(1)	(2)	(3)	(4)	(5)	(6)	(7)
90	.17264	14,160	2,445	12,938	58,667	4.14
91	.18718	11,715	2,192	10,619	45,729	3.90
92	.20243	9,523	1,928	8,558	35,110	3.69
93	.21750	7,595	1,652	6,769	26,552	3.50
94	.23186	5,943	1,378	5,255	19,783	3.33
95	.24584	4,565	1,122	4,003	14,528	3.18
96	.25854	3,443	890	2,998	10,525	3.06
97	.26980	2,553	689	2,209	7,527	2.95
98	.27996	1,864	522	1,603	5,318	2.85
99	.28949	1,342	388	1,148	3,715	2.77
100	.29836	954	285	811	2,567	2.69
101	.30659	669	205	566	1,756	2.62
102	.31420	464	146	391	1,190	2.56
103	.32122	318	102	268	799	2.51
104	.32768	216	71	180	531	2.46
105	.33361	145	48	121	351	2.42
106	.33904	97	33	80	230	2.38
107	.34401	64	22	53	150	2.34
108	.34855	42	15	35	97	2.30
109	.35269	27	9	23	62	2.27
110+	1.00000	18	18	39	39	2.17

Source: Modified from U.S. National Center for Health Statistics (1975, Table 3).

usually are somewhat lower than the age-specific death rates (M_x) that we have previously considered, but the rates are closely parallel. The technical question of how to derive a set of q_x values from a set of age-specific death rates need not concern us now.[4] It is necessary at this point to remember only that the q_x values are a set of mortality probabilities for the cohort as it begins each successive year of life.

Column 4: Number of Deaths between Age x and Age x + 1 (d$_x$)

To simplify our explanation, we discuss the fourth column of the life table before discussing the third column. The fourth column represents the number of deaths to the cohort between age x and age $x + 1$. Symbolized d_x, it is equal to the number surviving to exact age x (ℓ_x) multiplied by the probability of dying between age x and age $x + 1$:

$$d_x = (\ell_x)(q_x).$$

The number of cohort deaths (d_x) is also equal to the difference between the number surviving to age x and the number surviving to age $x + 1$; i.e.:

$$d_x = \ell_x - \ell_{x+1}$$

In Table 12, the number of deaths in the first year of life is 1,746, which is the product of 100,000 and .01746. The number of deaths at age 84 is 3,383, which is the product of 32,921 and .10275.

Column 3: Survivors at Exact Age x (ℓ_x)

The third column of the life table (ℓ_x) represents the number of people who have survived from birth to exact age x. The initial cohort, the radix, is 100,000 in Table 12 ($\ell_0 = 100,000$). In the first year of life, the probability of dying is .01746 (the value of q_0). Consequently, 1,746 persons of the original 100,000 die in the first year of life and only 98,254 persons reach exact age 1 ($\ell_1 = 98,254$).

The number of survivors to any age (ℓ_x) is equal to the product of ℓ_{x-1} and the value of the mortality rate for the preceding age interval (q_{x-1}), subtracted from the number who survived to the beginning of the preceding age interval (ℓ_{x-1}). In a formula:

$$\ell_x = \ell_{x-1} - [(q_{x-1})(\ell_{x-1})] = \ell_{x-1} - d_{x-1}.$$

---

4 Appendix 2 provides a brief introduction to the relationship between q_x values and M_x values for the interested reader.

To illustrate, we calculate the value of ℓ_x for exact age 19 for the life table in Table 12:

$$\ell_{19} = \ell_{18} - [(q_{18})(\ell_{18})]$$
$$= 97{,}467 - [(.00069)(97{,}467)]$$
$$= 97{,}467 - 67$$
$$= 97{,}400.$$

Lest these formulas be confusing, you should bear in mind that this is simply an algebraic statement of the fact that the number of survivors at any exact age consists of those alive one year earlier minus those who died during the intervening year.

The meaning of the ℓ_x column may be clearer if we refer to its possible use by an insurance company. In Table 12, note that 95,097 people reach age 40 and that 221 die during their 40th year. Suppose that the insurance company desires to provide $1,000 in term insurance for one year's coverage for each of the 95,097 people reaching age 40. Since 221 of the 95,097 are expected to die before their 41st birthday, $221,000 must be available to be paid out in benefits. The premium for the insurance is to be paid by 95,097 people; therefore each must pay in:

$$\frac{\$221{,}000}{95{,}097} = \$2.34 \text{ (plus any charges for administration or profits for the company).}$$

Column 5: Years Lived between Age x and Age x + 1 (L_x)

The fifth column of the life table (L_x) represents the number of person-years lived by the cohort during an age interval. Although an exact determination of L_x values is not usually possible, we can approximate the values by assuming that deaths are evenly distributed throughout the interval between age x and age $x + 1$ (except for the first few years of life). Making this assumption, we can estimate the value of L_x by averaging the number of survivors at the beginning of the age interval (ℓ_x) and the number of survivors at the end of the interval (ℓ_{x+1}). In other words, it is usually assumed that:

$$L_x = \frac{\ell_x + \ell_{x+1}}{2}.$$

This approximation makes use of the same logic as we used in our earlier discussion of the midyear population as an approximation of the number of person-years lived for calculating death rates.

For the first few years of life, it is not reasonable to use the average of ℓ_x and ℓ_{x+1} as an approximation of L_x because deaths are not evenly distributed throughout the year. Instead, they are concentrated at the earlier part of the year, as documented in our earlier discussion of the infant mortality rate. For this reason, values of L_x for the first few years should be closer to ℓ_{x+1} than to ℓ_x. In the absence of good data for estimating the relative weighting of ℓ_x and ℓ_{x+1}, it is often assumed that:

$$L_0 = .3\ell_0 + .7\ell_1$$
$$L_1 = .4\ell_1 + .6\ell_2.$$

For L_2 and for ages greater than 2, the $.5(\ell_x + \ell_{x+1})$ approximation is used. The formulas above are approximations based on empirical observations. When data are available on mortality of children by number of months since birth or by number of days since birth, more refined estimates of L_0 and L_1 are possible. We will not describe them here, but more sophisticated techniques are often used for calculating the L_x values for the first few years of life.[5]

Another way of looking at these observations is this: All the persons who survive the year (that is, live from ℓ_x to ℓ_{x+1}) live for one year. Therefore the minimum number of years lived is equal to ℓ_{x+1}. For example, all of the 94,876 people who live from age 40 to age 41 in Table 12 contribute one year of life; hence we begin with a minimum of 94,876 41-year-olds. In addition, the persons who die during that year (221 persons during the 40th year) live for some part of a year. If all of them were to die one second after their 40th birthday, then we could ignore the addition. On the other hand, if all the deaths occurred one second before the 41st birthday, we could assume that all the decedents lived a full year. Our assumption is that deaths are likely to be more or less evenly spaced throughout the year; if that is so, each decedent will have lived an average of one-half year; hence we add one-half of the deaths in the 40th year (110) to the total number alive at age 41 to obtain the total number of years lived between birthdays 40 and 41. The resulting number is 94,986. The logic of the life table permits us to make any other reasonable assumptions about the distribution of deaths during the

---

5 Such techniques have, in fact, been used in Table 12, which is why the values given for L_0 and L_1 are slightly different from what the above formulas would give.

year. Since we know that most infant deaths occur early in the first year of life, data on that first year are used to obtain an L_x figure that assumes much less than half a year of life for the infant decedents. When we approach the oldest ages of the age distribution, there may be similar effects.

Column 6: Total Years Lived after Exact Age x *(*T_x*)*

The sixth column of the life table gives the number of person-years lived after exact age x. We have already considered the number of years lived during the 40th year of life using the L_x column, which gives such figures for every particular year of life. The T_x figure at age 0 is the sum of all L_x entries—i.e., how many years will be lived in the first, second, third, etc., years of life when all are added together. The T_x figure for any other age (e.g., age 40) is the sum of the years lived (L_{40}) for that age and all later ages by those survivors still alive at the beginning of the age in question.

Thus, the entries in the sixth column show the number of person-years that the cohort will live *after* reaching age x; it is the sum of the values of L_x for age x and all ages greater than x that are presented in the life table. In a formula:

$$T_x = \sum_{i=x}^{w} L_i$$

where L_i = entry i in the L_x column, and

$\sum_{i=x}^{w} L_i$ means "take the sum of the L_x column starting with entry x and adding entries $x + 1$, $x + 2$, etc., until you have added the last entry (w)."

Column 7: Expectation of Life, or Average Number of Years Lived after Exact Age x *(*e_x*)*

The last column in the life table is one of the most commonly used. It answers the question: If all the persons alive at any age could share equally the total number of years that all will live from that year onward, how many years would each live on the average? After having calculated T_x (the total number of person-years lived after exact age x), and ℓ_x (the number of persons who survived to attain age x), it is easy to determine how long the average person in the life table lives after exact age x. We simply divide entries in the T_x column by entries in the ℓ_x column:

$$e_x = \frac{T_x}{\ell_x}$$

In the life table for U.S. females for 1969–71, women of exact age 35 had an expectation of living 42.28 more years on the average— that is, their expected time of death, on the average, was at exact age 77.28. Females of exact age 0, on the other hand, had an expectation of life of 74.64 years. Expressed informally, this means that women in the hypothetical cohort who survive the hazards of the first 35 years exhibit an increase in the average age to which they will live over the age expected at their birth.

The Abridged Life Table

The life table we have just described is known as a "complete" life table because it presents the life table functions for single years of age. There are also life tables that present the functions for groupings of years of age. They may refer, for example, to the probability of dying between exact age 5 and exact age 10 and present all the values in the table only for intervals of 5 years. In these "abridged" life tables, the first year of life and the ages from 1 to 4 are usually presented separately. Later ages are usually presented in five- or ten-year intervals. Although the calculation of the abridged table is different from that of the complete table, the interpretation of the values of the life table functions is the same as for the complete table. Only the time interval must be adjusted in discussions of values taken from an abridged table. A small number placed below and to the left of the letter for the life table function (e.g., $_5L_{10}$, $_4d_1$, or $_nq_x$) indicates the length of the interval. An abridged life table for U.S. females in 1978 is presented in Table 13.

Applications of the Life Table to Mortality Analysis

The life table functions provide useful tools for analyzing the effects of mortality alone because migration is explicitly excluded and fertility is held constant. The uses of the life table are many and varied, but we will concentrate on only three here: (1) uses of the stationary population concept, (2) survival ratios, and (3) comparisons of life expectancy at various ages.

The Stationary Population

The numbers in the L_x column may be thought of as similar to the

Table 13. Abridged life table for females: United States, 1978

Exact age in years	Interval in years	Probability of dying during age interval	Number of survivors at beginning of age interval	Number of deaths during age interval	Number of years lived between age x and age x+n	Total number of years lived after exact age x	Expectation of life (average number of years remaining at beginning of age interval)
x	n	$_nq_x$	ℓ_x	$_nd_x$	$_nL_x$	T_x	e_x
0	1	.0122	100,000	1,224	98,934	7,718,382	77.2
1	4	.0024	98,776	234	394,554	7,619,448	77.1
5	5	.0014	98,542	137	492,339	7,224,894	73.3
10	5	.0012	98,405	121	491,753	6,732,555	68.4
15	5	.0028	98,284	272	490,787	6,240,802	63.5
20	5	.0033	98,012	328	489,254	5,750,015	58.7
25	5	.0036	97,684	355	487,562	5,260,761	53.9
30	5	.0044	97,329	428	485,642	4,773,199	49.0
35	5	.0064	96,901	617	483,068	4,287,557	44.2
40	5	.0106	96,284	1,022	479,030	3,804,489	39.5
45	5	.0169	95,262	1,615	472,510	3,325,459	34.9
50	5	.0258	93,647	2,413	462,545	2,852,949	30.5
55	5	.0381	91,234	3,475	447,939	2,390,404	26.2
60	5	.0591	87,759	5,187	426,535	1,942,465	22.1
65	5	.0813	82,572	6,710	397,033	1,515,930	18.4
70	5	.1284	75,862	9,741	356,263	1,118,897	14.7
75	5	.2125	66,121	14,051	296,800	762,634	11.5
80	5	.3178	52,070	16,546	219,198	465,834	8.9
85	∞	1.0000	35,524	35,524	246,636	246,636	6.9

Source: U.S. National Center for Health Statistics (1980a, Table 5-1).

midyear population in each age group for a hypothetical or model population that demographers call the *stationary population*. The nature of this model population may be understood as resulting from the following process. Suppose that 100,000 persons are born each year and they are subject to the mortality rates shown in Table 12. After 40 years, the population would consist of all the age groups shown in the L_x column up through age 40. The persons shown at age 2 would be the survivors of the 100,000 babies born two years before, the persons in the 40th year would be the survivors of the 100,000 babies born 40 years previously, etc. After about 110 years, the whole population structure shown in the L_x column would have been created. From that time on—*ad infinitum*—the 100,000 entering the population at birth would be exactly balanced by the 100,00 dying at all ages. The size of this total population would be T_0, and the L_x column would give the age distribution of the stationary population.

The stationary population has many of the characteristics of a rea population. It has a crude birth rate,[6] called the "life table birth rate" and defined as follows:

$$b = k \frac{\ell_0}{T_0}$$

where ℓ_0 = the radix, usually 100,000
T_0 = the first entry of the T_x column, and
$k = 1,000$

Note again that T_0 is the total size of the stationary population, since it is the sum of all the values in the L_x column.

The stationary population also has a crude death rate, called the *life table death rate*. The life table death rate is equal to:

$$d = k \frac{\ell_0}{T_0}$$

or, alternatively, to the reciprocal of e_0 multiplied by a constant (i k/e_0). The life table death rate is the same as the life table birth rat of course, since everyone in the hypothetical cohort dies at some a This is one of the reasons why the hypothetical population is calle "stationary"—the number of births and the number of deaths are

---

6 Fertility measures are discussed in Chapter 3. The crude birth rate is the sa as the crude death rate except that the numerator for the crude birth rate the number of live births in a given year.

equal, and therefore the population is neither growing nor declining in size.

Earlier, we described the life table as the life history of a cohort of persons born (i.e., reaching exact age zero) during a single year who move through a series of mortality rates until all of them have died. Alternatively, we can think of the life table as describing what happens each year in a hypothetical stationary population. In talking about a stationary population, demographers look at it the following way:

> The stationary population is a model without immigration or emigration in which the same age-specific probabilities of death apply continuously and in which there are the same number of births and deaths each year (Greville, 1946: p. 21).

In a stationary population, the number of persons living in each age group never changes—because an individual who leaves an age group when he dies or becomes a year older is replaced by another individual from the next lower age group. The figures in the L_x column, as we have said, specify the age composition of this population.

Analytic Uses of the Stationary Population

The stationary population concept has limited descriptive value because the model of the life table is very different from what happens in a real population. It is useful for analytic purposes, however, because it summarizes what would be the age structure of a population subject to the fixed mortality and birth conditions in the life table. A comparison of the age composition of females in the United States in 1978 with that of the female stationary population for the same period shows, for example, that the stationary population is older than the actual population (Table 14). This reflects two facts: (1) mortality conditions for American females have improved,[7] and (2) crude birth rates have actually been higher than crude death rates, resulting, in the absence of migration, in a growing population and a young age distribution. A similar comparison would result if only the

---

7 Actually, falling mortality does not automatically make a population older or younger. The effect depends on the age pattern of the mortality changes. Historically, falling mortality has usually been especially important at the youngest ages, which has resulted in a younger population just as higher fertility does. Because infant and childhood mortality is now so low, future falls are likely to be concentrated at the older ages, and will result in an older population (all other factors equal).

Table 14. Age composition of the stationary population and the actual population for U.S. white females: 1978

Ages	Composition of stationary population[a]		Composition of actual population[b]		Difference between actual and stationary population percentage distributions (col. 4 minus col. 2)
	$_nL_x$	Percentage distribution of $_nL_x$	Estimated actual population on July 1, 1978, in thousands	Percentage distribution of actual population	
	(1)	(2)	(3)	(4)	(5)
<1	99,072	1.3	1,289	1.3	0.0
1–4	395,283	5.1	4,870	5.0	-0.1
5–9	493,314	6.3	6,815	7.1	+0.8
10–14	492,749	6.3	7,568	7.8	+1.5
15–19	491,793	6.3	8,718	9.0	+2.7
20–24	490,325	6.3	8,602	8.9	+2.6
25–29	488,818	6.3	7,741	8.0	+1.7
30–34	487,151	6.3	6,928	7.2	+0.9
35–39	484,938	6.2	5,781	6.0	-0.2
40–44	481,430	6.2	5,015	5.2	-1.0
45–49	475,598	6.1	5,077	5.3	-0.8
50–54	466,511	6.0	5,430	5.6	-0.4
55–59	452,973	5.8	5,265	5.4	-0.4
60–64	432,730	5.6	4,533	4.7	-0.9
65–69	404,187	5.2	4,252	4.4	-0.8
70–74	364,287	4.7	3,375	3.5	-1.2
75–79	305,546	3.9	2,356	2.4	-1.5
80–84	226,259	2.9	1,634	1.7	-1.2
85+	246,257	3.2	1,373	1.4	-1.8
All ages	7,779,221	100.0	96,622	99.9[c]	+0.0[c]

a   Source: U.S. National Center for Health Statistics (1980a, Table 5-1).

b   Source: U.S. Bureau of the Census (1980, Table 1).

c   Total percentage does not equal sum of column because of rounding.

latter condition were true—i.e., birth rates had been consistently higher than death rates.

Perhaps the most frequent use of the stationary population concept, however, is the comparison of the stationary population's death rates with those of the actual population. Table 15 presents life table

Table 15. Crude death rates and life table death rates for U.S. white
females: selected years, 1900–77

| Years | Rate | | Difference (life table rate minus crude rate) |
	Crude death rate	Life table death rate[a]	
1900–02	15.4[b]	19.6	+4.2
1909–11	13.2[b]	18.6	+5.4
1919–21	11.5[b]	17.1	+5.6
1929–31	9.9[b]	15.9	+6.0
1939–41	9.1[b]	14.9	+5.8
1949–51	8.0[b]	13.9	+5.9
1959–61	7.9[b]	13.5	+5.6
1968–70	9.5[c]	13.3	+3.8
1971–73	9.4[c]	13.2	+3.8
1974–76	9.0[d]	13.0	+4.0
1977	8.8[d]	12.9	+4.1

a Calculated by using U.S. National Center for Health Statistics (1980a, Table 5-5).

b Unweighted average of the three years. Sources: U.S. Bureau of the Census (1960:27);
   U.S. National Center for Health Statistics (1964:1–3).

c Source: United Nations Statistical Office, Department of Economic and Social Affairs,
   1972 *Demographic Yearbook* (1973, Table 23).

d Source: United Nations Statistical Office, Department of Economic and Social Affairs,
   1978 *Demographic Yearbook* (1979, Table 18).

death rates for white females in the United States for various periods
in the past 80 years and comparable figures for the crude death rates.
The life table death rates are consistently higher than the crude death
rates because the age composition of the actual population has been
much younger than the age composition of the stationary population.

Third Set of Multiple-Choice Questions

1. Life expectancy at birth for females in the United States is:
   (a) about 75 years.
   (b) about 35 years.
   (c) about 55 years.
   (d) about 100 years.

   What is the life expectancy at birth for females in your country?
   What is the life expectancy at birth for males in your country?

2. If the death rate of a stationary life table population is 10, this implies a life expectancy of about:
   (a) 65 years.
   (b) 50 years.
   (c) 100 years.
   (d) 30 years.
   (e) 10 years.

3. The difference between a generation life table and a period life table is that:
   (a) the radix is different.
   (b) one refers to a true birth cohort and the other does not.
   (c) one uses a different method for calculating q_0 than the other.
   (d) none of the above.

4. The life table mortality rates (q_x) are usually:
   (a) about the same as age-specific death rates (M_x).
   (b) higher than age-specific death rates (M_x).
   (c) exactly the same values as age-specific death rates (M_x).
   (d) lower than age-specific death rates (M_x).

5. If country A has a higher life expectancy than country B, but A has a higher crude death rate, it is likely that:
   (a) A's population is younger than that of B.
   (b) A's population is older than that of B.
   (c) A's population has a high infant mortality rate.
   (d) none of the above is probable.

6. In a country with a high life expectancy, the fact that the actual death rate is lower than the death rate of the stationary population means that:
   (a) the actual population is growing through natural increase.
   (b) the country has a younger actual population than the stationary population.
   (c) neither of the above is true.
   (d) (a) and (b) are both true.

Second Set of True-False Questions

Determine whether each of the following statements is true or false:

1. The life table death rate for females in the United States is higher than the crude death rate.

2. In a life table, the life table death rate is twice the life table birth rate.
3. A period life table is a hypothetical model because mortality rates actually change from one period to the next.
4. In a country where mortality rates have remained relatively constant for many years, a generation life table and a period life table would be almost identical.

Survival Ratios

The life table is particularly valuable for making population projections or for making estimates of population figures by age between census years. If we assume that the mortality conditions of a particular life table will continue in the future, we can determine what proportion of people in a given age group will survive from that particular age group to another. For most age groups in low mortality societies like the United States, this is a safe assumption. Death rates at most ages are so low and so stable that changes are not likely to be great. Even a considerable percentage change in death rates that are very low will make little difference in survival ratios. That is why population projections for a country like the United States are not likely to be seriously in error as a result of assumptions about future mortality rates. For example, since 93 percent of the women in the 1960 life table were surviving to age 45, projections for women less than 45 years of age could not be much affected by further reductions in mortality.

The L_x column specifies the midyear population of the stationary population in the age interval x to $x + 1$. If we want to determine the proportion of persons surviving from age group x to the later age group $x + n$, we simply determine:

$$\text{forward survival ratio from age } x \text{ to age } x + n = \frac{L_{x+n}}{L_x}.$$

On the other hand, if we want to know how many persons would have been alive n years in the past, we can determine:

$$\text{reverse survival ratio from age } x + n \text{ to age } x = \frac{L_x}{L_{x+n}}.$$

To illustrate this simply, suppose we have the life table of Table 12 and that it is the latest life table available. Government officials want to know how many females will be age 5 (i.e., between exact age 5 and exact age 6) in 1975 if there were roughly 2 million females of age 0 (not having reached their first birthday) in 1970. This information is needed, let us say, to determine how many girls will enter kindergarten in 1975. Using Table 12, we calculate:

$$\frac{L_5}{L_0} = \frac{97,934}{98,511} = 0.9941.$$

Using the life table, then, we estimate that 99.41 percent of the girls of age 0 in 1970 will survive to be age 5 in 1975. Multiplying by 2 million (the number of girls of age 0 in 1970), we estimate that there will be 1,988,200 females of age 5 in 1975, barring immigration and emigration of young children.

Another type of survival ratio introduced earlier is the ℓ_x column of the life table. The usefulness of this survival ratio is illustrated in the following paragraph.

Survival ratios vary dramatically from country to country and have changed rapidly in the less developed countries in a relatively short time span. Compare, for example, the survival ratios for males in Sri Lanka (formerly Ceylon) in 1920, 1946, 1954, and 1967 with those for white males in the United States in 1955 and 1978 (shown in Table 16). Whereas only 67 percent of the Sri Lankans born in 1920 would have survived to exact age 5 according to that life table, the figure was over 92 percent by 1967. United States ratios for 1955 and 1978 were even more favorable to survival. Since these survival ratios depend only on mortality (and exclude the effects of migration), they show that the mortality conditions in the two countries for the years shown were markedly different and that the Sri Lankan survival ratios improved significantly in the half century between 1920 and 1967.

Uses for the Life Expectancy Function in the Life Table

The e_x column of the life table is particularly useful. In comparing the mortality of two countries, we have seen that the death rates and even the standardized death rates have some weaknesses. Since the life expectancy figures in the life table are derived from a model that excludes migration and holds fertility constant, the values of the e_x function are often used to compare the mortality of different countries or the same country at several points in time.

The values of e_0, life expectancy at birth, are used especially often.

**Table 16. Survivors to exact age x (ℓ_x) of 100,000 male babies (ℓ_0):
Sri Lanka and United States, selected years**

Country and year	Age 0	Age 5	Age 20	Age 50	Age 65
Sri Lanka, 1920	100,000	67,167	56,681	34,458	19,174
Sri Lanka, 1946	100,000	75,448	70,089	51,963	33,245
Sri Lanka, 1954	100,000	86,948	84,332	76,085	62,541
Sri Lanka, 1967	100,000	92,472	90,584	81,651	66,697
United States, 1955 (white males)	100,000	96,906	95,743	87,044	65,704
United States, 1978 (white males)	100,000	98,383	97,275	89,693	71,073

Note: Sri Lanka was formerly known as Ceylon.

Sources: United Nations Statistical Office, Department of Economic and Social Affairs,
1957 *Demographic Yearbook* (1957, Table 26); 1974 *Demographic Yearbook* (1975,
Table 35); U.S. National Center for Health Statistics (1980a, Table 5-1).

Although the most accurate comparison of mortality in two countries would involve a detailed analysis of all the q_x values or all the
e_x values, the life expectancy at birth is a good summary measure. It
has some hazards, because the value of e_0 is disproportionately affected by the infant mortality rate, but infant mortality rates are
usually highly correlated with death rates at other ages. Further, the
value of e_0 has an immediately appealing interpretation: e_0 measures
how long members of a cohort can expect to live on the average if
mortality conditions remain the same in the future as they were during the year of birth.

In the 1960s and 1970s, values of life expectancy at birth ranged
among countries for which data were available from 37.0 to 73.0
years for males (Table 17). For females, who usually live longer than
males, the values ranged from 40.1 to 79.2 years.

Other illustrations of the use of life expectancy figures are shown
in Tables 18 and 19. From these tables, we can make the following
statements:

(1)   Males, regardless of color, had lower life expectancies than
      females at all ages in the United States in 1978 (Table 18).

(2)   Within each sex, nonwhites had lower life expectancies than
      whites at almost all ages in the United States in 1978 (Table
      18).

Table 17. Examples of high and low values of life expectancy at birth for males and females: recent years

Males			Females		
Country	Year or period	e_0	Country	Year or period	e_0
High					
Iceland	1975–76	73.0	Iceland	1975–76	79.2
Norway	1977–78	72.3	Norway	1977–78	78.7
Sweden	1974–78	72.2	Netherlands	1977	78.4
Netherlands	1977	72.0	Sweden	1974–78	78.1
Israel	1978	71.5	France	1977	77.9
Low					
Angola	1970–75	37.0	Angola	1970–75	40.1
Ethiopia	1970–75	37.0	Ethiopia	1970–75	40.1
Senegal	1970–75	39.4	Afghanistan	1970–75	40.7
Afghanistan	1970–75	39.9	Senegal	1970–75	42.5

Note: Some of the low values are based on U.N. estimates, because good registration data are lacking.

Source: United Nations Statistical Office, Department of Economic and Social Affairs, 1979 *Demographic Yearbook* (1980, Table 22).

Table 18. Life expectancies at selected exact ages for U.S. males and females, by color: 1978

Sex and color	Life expectancy at exact age:							
	0	10	20	30	40	50	60	70
Male								
White	70.2	61.5	52.0	42.8	33.6	24.8	17.2	11.1
Nonwhite	65.0	57.0	47.4	38.8	30.4	22.8	16.5	11.6
Female								
White	77.8	68.9	59.1	49.5	39.9	30.7	22.3	14.8
Nonwhite	73.6	65.4	55.6	46.2	37.0	28.5	21.2	14.8

Source: U.S. National Center for Health Statistics (1980a, Table 5-4).

(3) Life expectancy at birth increased substantially from 1850 to 1978 for both white males and white females. Life expectancy at age 40, however, increased only moderately. Life expectancy at age 70 hardly increased at all (Table 19).

The reader may find other comparisons that are of interest.

Table 19. Life expectancies for U.S. white males and females at exact ages 0, 40, and 70: 1850–1978

Year	White males, by age			White females, by age		
	0	40	70	0	40	70
1850	38.3	27.9	10.2	40.5	29.8	11.3
1890	42.5	27.4	9.4	44.5	28.8	10.2
1900–02	48.2	27.7	9.0	51.1	29.2	9.6
1901–10	49.3	27.6	8.9	52.5	29.3	9.5
1919–21	56.3	29.9	9.5	58.5	30.9	9.9
1920–29	57.8	29.4	9.2	60.6	31.0	9.7
1930–39	60.6	29.6	9.3	64.5	32.2	10.2
1939–41	62.8	30.0	9.4	67.3	33.3	10.5
1949–51	66.3	31.2	10.1	72.0	35.6	11.7
1959–61	67.6	31.7	10.3	74.2	37.1	12.4
1969–71	67.9	31.9	10.4	75.5	38.1	13.4
1976	69.7	33.1	10.9	77.3	39.5	14.4
1978	70.2	33.6	11.1	77.8	39.9	14.8

Note: Coverage is restricted to Massachusetts (1850, 1890), to death registration states (1900–29), and to the continental United States (1929–51).

Sources: 1850–1929: Dublin et al. (1949, Table 12); 1939–61: Grove and Hetzel (1968: 308); 1969–78: U.S. National Center for Health Statistics (1978a, Table 5-1; 1980a, Table 5-1; 1980b, Tables 2, 3).

Fourth Set of Multiple-Choice Questions

1. The stationary population is a model that:
   (a)   excludes migration.
   (b)   holds fertility constant.
   (c)   has fixed mortality rates.
   (d)   is not very good as a descriptive model and is mainly useful for analytic purposes.
   (e)   only (a), (b), and (c) are true.
   (f)   (a), (b), (c), and (d) are true.

2. Survival ratios may be used for:
   (a)   making projections of the future population.
   (b)   comparing the mortality of several countries or the same country at different points in time.
   (c)   estimating the effect of different levels of q_x on future population sizes.
   (d)   only (a) and (b).
   (e)   all (a), (b), and (c).

Third Set of True-False Questions

Determine whether each of the following statements is true or false:

1. Survival ratios from age 0 to age 1 are higher than other one-year survival ratios.
2. Life expectancy at age 70 has not increased very much in the United States in the past 130 years.
3. Life expectancy in the United States is greater for males than for females.
4. If you know the life expectancy at birth for a life table prepared for the year of your birth, you know how long you are going to live.
5. Standardized rates are almost always better measures of mortality than crude rates.
6. q_0 is usually larger than q_{10} and q_{70} is usually larger than q_{40}.

Additional Reading

For further reading on the materials in this chapter, the following are good sources:

George W. Barclay, *Techniques of Population Analysis* (New York: John Wiley and Sons, Inc., 1958).

A.J. Jaffe, *Handbook of Statistical Methods for Demographers* (Washington, D.C.: U.S. Bureau of the Census, 1951).

Warren S. Thompson and David T. Lewis, *Population Problems,* fifth edition (New York: McGraw-Hill Book Co., 1965), especially chapter 12.

L.I. Dublin, A.J. Lotka, and M. Spiegelman, *Length of Life,* revised edition (New York: Ronald Press, 1949).

More advanced discussion of the material in the *Guide* can be found in such books as the following:

Mortimer Spiegelman, *Introduction to Demography,* revised edition (Cambridge, Massachusetts: Harvard University Press, 1968).

Nathan Keyfitz, *Introduction to the Mathematics of Population* (Reading, Massachusetts: Addison-Wesley Co., 1968).

Hugh H. Wolfenden, *Population Statistics and Their Compilation,* revised edition (Chicago: University of Chicago Press, 1954).

Henry S. Shryock, Jacob S. Siegel, and Associates, *The Methods and Materials of Demography* (Washington, D.C.: U.S. Bureau of the Census, U.S. Government Printing Office, 1971), 2 vols. (Condensed version available from Academic Press, New York, 1978)

Roland Pressat, *Demographic Analysis: Methods, Results, Applications* (New York: Aldine-Atherton, 1972).

For data on mortality for many nations and for many time periods, we found the following sources of particular value:

Nathan Keyfitz and Wilhelm Flieger, *World Population: An Analysis of Vital Data* (Chicago: University of Chicago Press, 1968).

Nathan Keyfitz and Wilhelm Flieger, *Population: Facts and Methods of Demography* (San Francisco: W.H. Freeman and Co., 1971).

Samuel H. Preston, Nathan Keyfitz, and Robert Schoen, *Causes of Death: Life Tables for National Populations* (New York: Seminar Press, 1972).

United Nations Statistical Office, Department of Economic and Social Affairs, *United Nations Demographic Yearbook,* published annually (various issues), and Population Bulletin No. 6, *The Situation and Recent Trends of Mortality in the World* (1962).

Illustrations of the wide utility of the measures discussed in the guide can be found by referring to studies of mortality in such sources as:

Richard A. Easterlin, ed., *Population and Economic Change in Developing Countries* (Chicago: University of Chicago Press, 1980).

Samuel H. Preston, ed., *The Effects of Infant and Child Mortality on Fecundity* (New York: Academic Press, 1978).

Samuel H. Preston, *Mortality Patterns in National Populations* (New York: Academic Press, 1976).

For an interesting discussion using only the most basic mortality measures, the following United Nations publication is recommended:

United Nations Population Division, Department of Social Affairs, *The Determinants and Consequences of Population Trends,* Population Studies No. 50 (New York: 1973).

Fertility, Natural Increase, and Reproduction Rates   3

At the beginning of the last chapter, we noted the importance of mortality as a determinant of population growth for most of human history. In more recent history, fertility and fertility control have become dominant in population policy and demographic interest. To illustrate the facts that prompted the shift in attention, in 1980 there were roughly 76 million more births than deaths in the world, and the ratio of births to deaths was more than two to one. The increases in population due to these "natural" processes of birth and death (natural increase) led many concerned nations in the 1960s and 1970s to adopt national programs for fertility control—just as in the past they had emphasized death control through campaigns against the plague, malaria, tuberculosis, polio, and other diseases.

In this chapter we examine the more common measures of fertility and natural increase used in the recent literature. In studying these measures, you will note that most of them are rates, and consequently we follow some of the same procedures as used in measuring mortality. For example, we talk about crude rates, specific rates, and standardized rates. There are also some special problems in the measurement of fertility, however. We discuss these before describing particular rates.

Special Problems in Measuring Fertility

Fertility measures always relate the number of live births to a specific population base and time reference period. Unfortunately, it is difficult to establish accurate statistical records on live births because many infants die in the first few moments after birth or in the first few days of infancy. A definition that exactly describes a live birth is difficult to establish, and once established it is difficult to be certain that any complex definition is actually used by local registration authorities. An internationally approved definition of a *live birth* is as follows:

> A live birth is the complete expulsion or extraction from its mother of a product of conception, irrespective of the duration of pregnancy, which, after such separation, breathes or shows any other evidence of life, such as beating of the heart, pulsation of the umbilical cord, or definite movement of voluntary muscles, whether or not the umbilical cord has been cut or the placenta is attached; each product of such a birth is considered live born (United Nations Statistical Office, 1955: p. 6).

It is unlikely that this definition is followed everywhere in all cases. When a child dies before the birth is registered, it is easily possible for neither the birth nor the death to be registered, only one or the other to be registered, or the birth to be registered as a stillbirth. The registration system is thus prone to error. Similarly, when a survey respondent is asked to report in retrospect on live births, such short-lived children are particularly apt to be omitted.

Fertility measurement also presents special problems not encountered with mortality measurement because a woman can die only once but she may have no births or more than one birth. This distinction between mortality and fertility allows us to consider two approaches to fertility measurement: the cumulative fertility approach and the vital rates (or yearly birth rates) approach. In using the cumulative fertility approach, we measure the average number of children ever born to women up to some specified age of the parents. In using the vital rates approach, we measure the number of live births in a given year as related to the population exposed to the "risk" of giving birth in that year.

The vital rates in fertility measurement are most similar to the mortality rates discussed in the first chapter, but even here there are important differences. The population exposed to the risk of childbearing is not ordinarily decreased by having a birth. Dying, on the other hand, completely removes a person from the population exposed to the risk of dying. Moreover, plural births (e.g., twins or triplets) are possible even though infrequent.

Fertility measurement is also complicated by the fact that fertility involves two parents, whereas death involves only one person. The fact that a couple is the base is problematic when we want to

consider specific rates, because we have to decide whose characteristics to use, the father's or the mother's.

Another problem is that not every woman is truly exposed to the
risk of childbearing, for the reason that not every woman in the population is paired with a member of the opposite sex. In addition,
through widowhood, divorce, separation, and the like, individuals
may enter or leave a couple unit at various times in their lives. There
are also minimum and maximum ages at which men and women are
physiologically capable of reproduction.[1]

Because of these special problems in measuring fertility, no one
measurement system comparable to the life table has become dominant in fertility studies. Instead, there is a wide variety of rates and
ratios in current use, each of which has advantages and limitations in
particular analytic situations.

The Crude Birth Rate

The *crude birth rate* (CBR) is defined as the number of births in a
given year divided by the number of people in the population in the
middle of that year.[2] The rate is usually expressed per 1,000 persons.
In a formula, we have:

$$\text{CBR} = 1,000 \left[\frac{\text{number of births}}{\text{midyear population}}\right] = k\frac{B}{P}.$$

Around the mid-1970s, the range of crude birth rates for major countries of the world was 9 to 51 births per 1,000 per annum. The highest recorded rates were found in Africa, Central and South America,
and Asia. The lowest recorded rates were found in Europe (Table 20).
Ninety-two percent of the more developed nations had rates under
25 whereas 78 percent of the less developed nations had rates of over
35 (Table 21). Although the crude birth rate is not a refined measure
of fertility, most other fertility measures show this pattern of higher
rates in the developing world.

---

1 It is conventional among demographers to distinguish between fertility and
fecundity. Fertility refers to actual reproductive performance, whereas fecundity refers to the physiological capacity of a man, woman, or couple to reproduce (United Nations Statistical Office, 1958: p. 38).

2 Again, as in the CDR, the ideal denominator is number of person-years lived,
which is just about impossible to calculate for a real population.

Table 20. Highest and lowest crude birth rates, by region: recent
           years

Region and country	Year or period	Crude birth rates (per 1,000)	
		High	Low
Africa			
Niger	1974	50.8	
Kenya	1974	50.5	
South Africa (white population)	1975		18.9
Egypt	1978		37.4
Central and North America			
Haiti	1974	49.7	
Honduras	1974	48.6	
Canada	1978		15.3
United States	1978		15.3
South America			
Bolivia	1975	46.6	
Ecuador	1974	42.2	
Uruguay	1977		20.4
Chile	1976		23.9
Asia			
Saudi Arabia	1975	49.5	
Yemen	1975	48.7	
Singapore	1978		16.9
Hong Kong	1978		17.6
Europe			
Albania	1970–75	31.9	
Ireland	1978	21.1	
Germany, Federal Republic	1978		9.4
Austria	1978		11.3
Oceania			
Papua New Guinea	1970–75	42.0	
Australia	1978		15.8

Note: Many of these rates are estimates and vary in reliability. Countries with populations of
    less than 1 million are excluded.

Source: United Nations Statistical Office, Department of Economic and Social Affairs,
    1978 and 1979 *Demographic Yearbooks* (1979 and 1980, Tables 9).

Table 21. Distribution of countries, by level of crude birth rate: 1974–78

Crude birth rate (per 1,000 population)	World total	Less developed regions	More developed regions	Africa	Asia (excluding U.S.S.R.)	South America	Europe (excluding U.S.S.R.)	North America	Oceania	U.S.S.R.
All countries	127	91	36	39	33	10	26	15	3	1
<15.0	15		15				15			
15.0–19.9	17		17		3		9	2	2	1
20.0–24.9	4	3	1			2	1	1		
25.0–29.9	10	9	1		5	1		4		
30.0–34.9	9	8	1		5	1	1	2		
35.0–39.9	13	13		4	4	4		1		
40.0–44.9	16	15	1	4	7	1		3	1	
45.0–49.9	37	37		26	8	1		2		
50.0–54.9	6	6		5	1					
55.0+										

Note: Countries with populations of less than 1 million are excluded.

Source: United Nations Statistical Office, Department of Economic and Social Affairs, 1978 *Demographic Yearbook* (1979, Table 9).

The Crude Rate of Natural Increase

As one might imagine from the recent concern about the "population explosion," typical values of the crude birth rate are higher than typical values of the crude death rate. The crude rate of natural increase measures this gap, as in the following formula:

$$\text{CRNI} = 1,000 \ [\frac{\text{number of births} - \text{number of deaths}}{\text{midyear population}}]$$

$$= k\frac{B-D}{P} = [k\frac{B}{P}] - [k\frac{D}{P}]$$

$$= \text{crude birth rate} - \text{crude death rate.}$$

In the 1970–75 period, the population of the world had a crude rate of natural increase around 18 per 1,000 (Table 22). The nations with the highest rates (21 to 32) were those in the developing regions: most of Africa, all of Latin America except for the temperate region, and South Asia. Europe, the U.S.S.R., and North America had the lowest rates (3 to 9). Middle Africa, temperate South America, East Asia, and Oceania had intermediate rates (13 to 24). Of course, any positive rate of natural increase, in the absence of net migration, if continued would lead to very large populations over time. Using the compound interest formula and compounding annually, even a yearly natural increase rate of only 5 per 1,000 would quadruple a population in less than 300 years. At the high natural increase rate of 30, which is found in much of the developing world, a population doubles in only 24 years, triples in 38 years, and quadruples in 47 years (Table 23).

The natural increase rates of recent decades are very high compared with those of previous historical periods. Using the data for all regions from Table 24, we have estimated the crude rates of natural increase for the period from 1650 to 1978 to be as follows:

Years	Annual crude rate of natural increase (per 1,000)
1650–1750	3.7
1750–1850	4.7
1850–1900	5.4
1900–50	8.4
1950–60	18.6
1960–70	19.5
1970–78	18.3

Table 22. Average crude rates of natural increase, by region: 1970–75

Region	Crude rate of natural increase
Africa, total	27
West Africa	30
East Africa	28
North Africa	25
Middle Africa	24
Southern Africa	26
North America, total	9
Latin America, total	26
Tropical South America	28
Middle America (mainland)	32
Temperate South America	13
Caribbean	21
Asia, total (excluding U.S.S.R.)	21
East Asia	16
South Asia	25
Europe, total (excluding U.S.S.R.)	6
Western Europe	6
Southern Europe	9
Eastern Europe	6
Northern Europe	3
Oceania, total	18
U.S.S.R.	8
All regions	18

Note: Many of these rates are estimates and vary in reliability.

Source: United Nations Statistical Office, Department of Economic and Social Affairs, 1978 *Demographic Yearbook* (1979, Table 1).

We calculated these rates by presuming natural increase to be constant and by using the exponential growth formula:

$$\frac{P_2}{P_1} = e^{rt}$$

where: P_2 = population at time 2,

P_1 = population at time 1,

Table 23. **Approximate number of years a population takes to double, triple, and quadruple in size, given specified rates of growth**

(Based on the compound interest formula of $P_n = P_0(1+r)^n$)

Rate (%) of growth per annum (r)	Double in size	Triple in size	Quadruple in size
	Approximate number of years (n) population takes to:		
0.5	139	220	278
0.7	99	158	199
1.0	70	111	139
1.2	58	92	116
1.5	47	74	93
1.7	41	65	83
2.0	35	55	70
2.2	32	51	64
2.5	28	45	56
2.7	26	42	52
3.0	24	38	47
3.2	22	35	44
3.5	21	32	41
3.7	19	31	38
4.0	18	28	35

Note: The crude rate of natural increase per 1,000 is equivalent to 10 times the percentage rate used here. For example, a rate of 0.5 percent is equivalent to a crude rate of natural increase of 5 per 1,000; similarly, an increase of 4 percent per annum (or .04) is equivalent to a crude rate of natural increase of 40 per 1,000.

Source: Marty and Neebe (1966:1–8).

r = the growth rate,

t = the number of years, and

e = base of natural logarithms (e = 2.71828282 . . .).

For example, the growth rate for 1650–1750 can be calculated by making $P_2 = 791$, $P_1 = 545$, and $t = 100$. Hence:

$$\frac{791}{545} = e^{100r}.$$

Solving the equation yields a growth rate of approximately 3.7 per 1,000. From these estimates, it is clear that the rate of growth has been much higher from 1950 to the present than it ever was

Table 24. Estimates of mid-year population, by region: selected years, 1650–1978

Population and region	1650	1750	1850	1900	1950	1960	1970	1978
Millions of persons								
Europe[a]	100	167	284	430	572	639	704	742
North America	1	2	26	82	166	199	226	242
Central and South America	12	16	38	74	164[b]	215[b]	283[b]	349[b]
Oceania	2	2	2	6	13	16	19	22
Africa	100	106	111	133	219	275	354	442
Asia	330	498	801	925	1,380	1,683	2,091	2,461
All regions	545	791	1,262	1,650	2,513	3,027	3,678	4,258
Percentage distribution								
Europe[a]	18.3	21.0	22.5	26.1	22.8	21.1	19.1	17.4
North America	0.2	0.3	2.1	5.0	6.6	6.6	6.1	5.7
Central and South America	2.2	2.0	3.0	4.5	6.5	7.1	7.7	8.2
Oceania	0.4	0.3	0.1	0.0	0.5	0.5	0.5	0.5
Africa	18.3	13.4	8.8	8.1	8.7	9.1	9.6	10.4
Asia	60.6	63.0	63.5	56.1	54.9	55.6	56.9	57.8
All regions	100.0	100.0	100.0	100.0	100.0	100.0	100.0[c]	100.0

a Includes Asiatic portions of U.S.S.R.

b Includes Caribbean.

c Column does not add exactly to 100.0 percent because of rounding.

Sources: 1650: Carr-Saunders (1936:42). 1750–1900: Durand (1968:109). 1950–78: United Nations Statistical Office, Department of Economic and Social Affairs, 1978 Demographic Yearbook (1979, Table 1).

previously. While death rates have declined to low or moderate levels for much of the world's population, birth rates have remained relatively high. It is this fact that has led to concern about the "population explosion" and to such dramatic (and admittedly unlikely) projections as the following:

> Projection of the post-World War II rate of increase gives a population of one person per square foot of the land surface of the earth in less than 800 years. It gives a population of 50 billion (the highest estimate of the population-carrying capacity of the globe ever calculated by a responsible scholar) in less than 200 years (Hauser, 1960: p. 7).

Because of projections like this, the crude rate of natural increase has been an important and recurrent measure in recent demographic literature.

The General Fertility Rate

In the mortality chapter, we discussed the rationale for using age-specific death rates or death rates specific for other characteristics. Fertility is also highly variable within subgroups of a population, and it is common to calculate age-specific, age-marital-status-specific, and other specific fertility rates.

The relative frequency of childbirth varies significantly with the age of the parents, and the age at which maximum fertility occurs may be different for the male and the female. Furthermore, fertility is higher among couples who have established some type of regular cohabitation (legal marriage or common-law marriage, for example) than among persons not in such unions (single persons, for example). Conventionally, specific fertility rates are given for female parents and not male parents, and henceforth we will discuss specific birth rates for females only; male parallels could be developed in each case.

It is rare for a child to be born to a woman less than 15 years old or more than 50 years old. For this reason, one may refine the measurement of fertility somewhat by using the midyear population of women in the childbearing years for the denominator of the rate instead of the total midyear population. The rate so constructed is called the age-delimited or *general fertility rate* (GFR). It is defined as the number of births in a given year divided by the midyear population of women in the age groups 15—44 or 15—49, although the ages 10—49 are sometimes used. In a formula:

$$\text{GFR} = 1{,}000 \; [\frac{\text{number of births in a given year}}{\substack{\text{midyear population of women} \\ \text{of ages } 15-44 \text{ or } 15-49}}]$$

$$= k \, \frac{B}{{}_{30}P^f_{15}} \; \text{ or } \; k \, \frac{B}{{}_{35}P^f_{15}}.$$

The purpose of the GFR is to restrict the denominator to potential mothers, but it is not restrictive enough for careful analysis. The values of rates within five-year age groups may be different for two populations and yet they may have the same general fertility rate if the age composition of women in the childbearing years differs for the two populations. In this sense, the GFR is subject to the same kind of crudeness as the crude birth rate, although it is a distinct improvement in precision.

In the recent past, general fertility rates for various countries have been in the range of the low 60s to the middle 200s. Estimates for the year 1960 prepared by Cho (1964) show that the highest values of GFR were 234.8 for the Sudan and 234.4 for Brunei. The lowest values were 61.1 for Sweden and 62.2 for Japan. As is true of the crude birth rate, the highest rates were found in the developing world and the lowest rates were usually found in Europe.

Age-Specific Fertility Rates

Within the age range of 15–49 years, there are marked differences in the fertility of women of different ages. For this reason, it is customary to calculate fertility rates for each age or age group, as in the following formula:

$${}_nF_x = \begin{array}{l}\text{Age-specific fertility} \\ \text{rate for age group} \\ x, \, x+n\end{array} = 1{,}000 \; \frac{\substack{\text{number of births to women} \\ \text{in age group } x, \, x+n}}{\substack{\text{midyear population of women} \\ \text{in age group } x, \, x+n}}$$

$${}_nF_x = k \, \frac{{}_nB_x}{{}_nP^f_x}$$

where ${}_nB_x$ = births to women of the age group $x, \, x+n$

${}_nP^f_x$ = midyear population of women in the group $x, \, x+n$, and

k = 1,000.

In most analyses, five-year age groups are used to calculate the age-specific rates. Typically, the age-specific rates are low or moderate in the 15—19 age group, highest in the twenties, and then decline to moderate levels for women in their thirties. Rates after age 39 are usually low. Rates in 1970—71 for China (Taiwan), the United States, and Sweden are portrayed graphically in Figure 2 to illustrate the typical, mountain-shaped patterns of age-specific fertility. Described more formally, the typical distribution is truncated, positively skewed, and leptokurtic relative to a normal distribution.

Although the patterns of age-specific rates are reasonably similar for different populations, the absolute levels of the age-specific rates vary considerably. Table 25 presents lowest and highest age-specific rates by age group, based on estimates by Palmore (1978) for major nations in the 1970s. Among selected groups of women, even higher age-specific rates have been recorded. An example often cited to il-lustrate very high fertility is the schedule of age-specific rates for the ethnic Hutterites of North America, an Anabaptist religious sect liv-ing in the United States and Canada in small colonies. In their book *Man's Capacity to Reproduce: The Demography of a Unique Popu-lation,* Eaton and Mayer (1954) reported the age-specific fertility rates for the Hutterite women in the 1936—40 period. Table 26 com-pares the Hutterite rates with the rates for all U.S. women in 1940. At all ages except for ages 15—19, the Hutterite rates were dramati-cally higher than the rates for all U.S. women. (The reason the Hut-terite rates were lower at ages 15—19 is that Hutterites practice relatively late marriage.) These figures mean that during the peak

Table 25. Lowest and highest age-specific fertility rates (ASFRs) per 1,000 women: 1970s

Women's ages	Lowest			Highest	
	Rate	Country		Rate	Country
15—19	4	Japan		228	Turkey
20—24	120	Finland		362	Algeria
25—29	66	Dem. Rep. of Germany		370	Syria
30—34	39	Dem. Rep. of Germany		347	Iraq
35—39	17	Bulgaria		281	Iraq
40—44	3	Japan		157	Libya
45—49	0	Japan		46	Tunisia

Source: Palmore (1978, Table 4).

Figure 2. Age-specific fertility rates for China (Taiwan), the United States, and Sweden: 1970—71

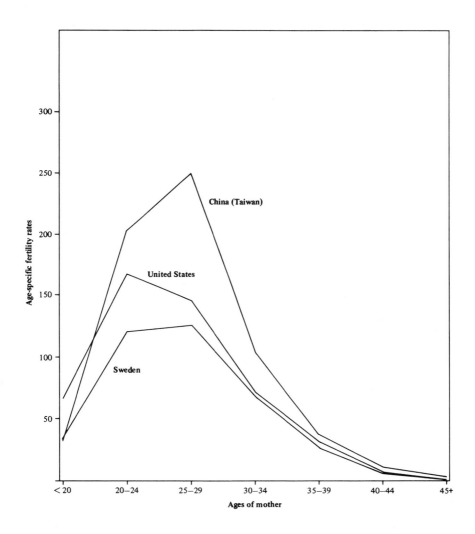

**Table 26. Age-specific fertility rates per 1,000 women: Hutterites
and all U.S. women, around 1940**

Women's ages	Hutterite women, 1936–40	U.S. women, 1940[a]
15–19	13	54
20–24	259	136
25–29	466	123
30–34	462	83
35–39	431	46
40–44	203	16
45–49	48	2

a   U.S. rates have been corrected for underregistration of births.

Sources: Hutterite women: Eaton and Mayer (1954, Table 11). U.S. women: U.S. National
Center for Health Statistics (1978b, Table 1-6).

fertility years, roughly 46 percent of the Hutterite women gave
birth each year (46.2 percent for women of ages 30–34 and 46.6
percent for women 25–29). Even as late as ages 35–39, 43 percent
gave birth each year.

The Hutterite rates and the ranges cited from Palmore's estimates
are examples of the extremes in age-specific rates. Most of the rates
in any age group are much closer together. At ages 15–19, 69 percent of the age-specific rates in Palmore's estimates are in the range
of 50–149. At ages 20–24, 67 percent of the age-specific rates are in
the range 200–349. Most of the rates in the remaining age groups
show similar patterns of concentration in a narrow range (Table 27).

Fourth Set of True-False Questions

Determine whether each of the following statements is true or false:

1. As a result of postwar progress, only about one-half of the world's
   population lives in countries with high rates of natural increase;
   the other half has attained relatively low rates of natural increase
   resulting from low birth rates and low death rates.
2. The majority of countries in the 1960s and 1970s had crude birth
   rates above 35 per thousand per annum.
3. The recent crude rate of natural increase for the population of the
   world was never attained in the period between 1650 and 1950.
4. It is unlikely that a population would have a crude birth rate of 40
   and a crude death rate of 15 during the same period.

Table 27. Distribution of major countries and territories, by level of age-specific fertility rates

Ages of women	Level of age-specific fertility rates (per 1,000)								All levels
	0–49	50–99	100–149	150–199	200–249	250–299	300–349	350–362	
Number of countries									
15–19	28	43	49	12	1	0	0	0	133
20–24	0	0	18	23	16	45	28	3	133
25–29	0	0	20	23	25	43	20	2	133
30–34	2	23	17	15	38	28	9	1	133
35–39	29	16	11	37	29	11	0	0	133
40–44	52	27	52	2	0	0	0	0	133
45–49	132	1	0	0	0	0	0	0	133
Percentage distribution (%)									
15–19	21	32	37	9	1	0	0	0	100
20–24	0	0	14	17	12	34	21	2	100
25–29	0	0	15	17	19	32	15	2	100
30–34	2	17	13	11	29	21	7	1	100
35–39	22	12	8	28	22	8	0	0	100
40–44	39	20	39	2	0	0	0	0	100
45–49	99	1	0	0	0	0	0	0	100

Note: Estimates are based on recent data. Percentages do not add exactly to 100 percent because of rounding.

Source: Palmore (1978, Table 4).

5. The lowest birth rates recorded in the 1970s were for the European nations.

Fifth Set of Multiple-Choice Questions

1. In two countries, A and B, the age-specific fertility rates for females are as follows:

Ages	Country A	Country B
15–24 years	80	80
25–34 years	250	250
35–44 years	100	100

   (a)   Country A has a higher general fertility rate than country B.
   (b)   Country B has a higher general fertility rate than country A.
   (c)   Country A has the same general fertility rate as country B.
   (d)   Country A has the same crude birth rate as country B.
   (e)   The general fertility rate for country A may be the same, higher, or lower than the general fertility rate for country B.

2. The crude birth rate in the United States is now approximately:
   (a)   10 per thousand.
   (b)   15 per thousand.
   (c)   25 per thousand.
   (d)   35 per thousand.
What is the crude birth rate in your own country?

3. Characterize as closely as possible the population of the United States, Canada, and the U.S.S.R.
   (a)   crude birth rate of 21–44, crude death rate of 20–30.
   (b)   crude birth rate of 15–20, crude death rate of 5–10.
   (c)   crude birth rate of 20–30, crude death rate of 15–25.
   (d)   crude birth rate of 9–34, crude death rate of 5–20.
   (e)   crude birth rate of 10–16, crude death rate of 5–30.

4. Characterize as closely as possible the populations of the European nations.
(Select from the same answer categories as for question 3.)

5. A crude rate of natural increase of 30 per thousand leads to a doubling of the population in approximately:
   (a)   15 years.
   (b)   25 years.
   (c)   50 years.

(d)   75 years.

(e)   100 years.

6. Typically, age-specific fertility rates for women:

   (a)   are highest at ages 15−24 and lower thereafter.

   (b)   are highest at ages 20−29 and lower at ages 15−19 and ages over 30.

   (c)   are highest at ages 25−34 and lowest at ages 15−24 and ages over 35.

   (d)   are fairly constant throughout the childbearing years.

Birth Rates Specific for Characteristics Other Than Age

It is often desirable to study birth rates specific for characteristics other than age. Two important characteristics are marital status and live birth order.

All societies have some form of culturally sanctioned reproductive unit resulting from a religious marriage, legal marriage, consensual union, common-law marriage, or other union.[3] For convenience, we call all of these institutionalized arrangements "marriage" in the present discussion. Although marriage is a nearly universal phenomenon, there is significant variation in norms about the proper age to marry, about remarriage of widows, and about divorce. The norms may change over time and the possibility of adhering to them may be affected by the age and sex composition of the population. For example, in populations where there is a shortage of eligible males or females, persons of the opposite sex who wish to marry may find themselves caught in a "marriage squeeze." (For a discussion of this phenomenon, see Akers, 1967.) Since the proportions married may vary, and since birth rates generally are much higher for the married than for the total population of women, it is useful to construct fertility rates specific for marital status as well as for age, so that one has age-marital-status-specific fertility rates.

Four articles by Freedman and Adlakha (1968), Cho et al. (1968), Cho and Hahm (1968), and Retherford and Cho (1973) illustrate the use of fertility rates specific for age and marital status. The articles examine the factors responsible for declining crude birth rates in Hong Kong, West Malaysia, the Republic of Korea, and East Asia. To quote Freedman and Adlakha (p. 181):

3   For an informative discussion of the complexity of marital unions in relation to fertility, see Stycos and Back (1964, especially Chapters 4−6).

An important question about such declines in crude birth rates is whether they result from real declines in the fertility of married women or from changes in the number of women of childbearing age or in the proportion who are married in the productive childbearing years. Are married women having fewer children or are there simply fewer married women in the important childbearing years?

Although we cannot review the details here, changes in the marital status composition of the populations were among the causes of declining birth rates in all four cases. In addition, changes in the age composition were important for Hong Kong in the 1961—65 period but not in 1965—66. For Korea and West Malaysia, changes in the age structure were less important in the declines. There were also genuine declines in age-specific rates among married women in all three countries. The Retherford and Cho article summarizes more recent evidence. Declines in the crude birth rates reported there were due both to real declines in marital fertility and to changes in the age and marital status composition of the population.

Fertility rates specific for live birth order are also useful. The probability of having an additional child is affected by how many children a woman has already borne. This is true because contraception may be used after a certain number of births and because the physiological capacity to bear children is affected by previous childbirths as well as by age and other factors. One may calculate the rates as follows:

$$\begin{matrix} \text{Birth order-specific} \\ \text{fertility rate} \end{matrix} = 1{,}000 \left[\frac{\text{number of births of order } i}{\begin{matrix} \text{midyear population of women} \\ \text{of ages } 15-44 \text{ or } 15-49 \end{matrix}} \right]$$

$$= k \frac{B^i}{{}_{30}P^f_{15}} \text{ or } k \frac{B^i}{{}_{35}P^f_{15}}$$

where B^i = births of order i,

$_{30}P^f_{15}$ or $_{35}P^f_{15}$ = midyear population of women between the ages of 15—44 or 15—49, and

k = 1,000.

(Note that the sum of the birth order-specific fertility rates is the GFR.) It is often useful to make the rates specific for smaller age groups, and we may calculate age- and birth order-specific fertility rates.

To illustrate the use of rates specific for live birth order, we will consider the data for the United States summarized in Table 28. The general fertility rate in the United States was lower in 1975 (66.7) than in 1942 (91.5). During the intervening 33 years, the rate had both increased and decreased from the 1942 level, reaching a high value of 122.9 in 1957 and thereafter declining fairly steadily to the 1975 level of 66.7. Table 28 shows data for two of the intervening years, 1960 and 1967.

Rates for all birth orders but the first were higher in 1960 than in 1942. The 1960 first-birth order birth rate was low because so many women had already had first children in the "baby boom" period of the 1950s. Most of the difference in the general fertility rates of 1960 and 1942 (118.0 – 91.5 = 26.5) resulted from higher rates for second, third, and fourth births (25.2 of the 26.5 difference). It is also noteworthy that whereas the general fertility rate was about the same in 1942 and 1967, the birth rates by birth order were significantly different. The fall in the GFR between 1960 and 1967 continued to 1975. Much of the 1960–75 fall (118.0 – 66.7 = 51.3) was due to declines in the rates for the third and fourth birth orders (total fall of 24.0), but the rates fell for all orders during the period.

Fertility rates specific for age, for marital status, or for live birth order are only three examples of many specific rates that may be useful in a particular fertility analysis. Demographers may also be interested in the variation in fertility rates by parity of mother, educational attainment, income, size of place of residence, ethnic group, occupation, contraceptive use, and other social and economic variables. The method of computing rates specific for other characteristics is similar to that examined for age, marital status, and live birth order.

Standardized Birth Rates

Because we are interested in measuring fertility, we often want to control for the effect of other variables. We may look at a detailed schedule of specific fertility rates (by age, marital status, or any other characteristic) and compare two populations in this way. Alternatively, we may want a single measure that corrects for the effects of the extraneous variables. One such measure would be a standardized fertility rate, corresponding to the standardized mortality rates previously discussed.

The most common standardized fertility measure in use is the

Table 28. Birth rates by live birth order and percentage change in rates: United States, selected years, 1942–75

Live birth order	Live births per 1,000 women 15–44 years old				Percentage change[a]				
	1942 (1)	1960 (2)	1967 (3)	1975 (4)	1942–60 (5)	1960–67 (6)	1967–75 (7)	1942–67 (8)	1942–75 (9)
First birth	37.5	31.1	30.8	28.4	–17.1	–1.0	–7.8	–17.9	–24.3
Second birth	22.9	29.2	22.6	21.2	27.5	–22.6	–6.2	–1.3	–7.4
Third birth	11.9	22.8	13.9	9.5	91.6	–39.0	–31.6	16.8	–20.2
Fourth birth	6.6	14.6	8.3	3.9	121.2	–43.2	–53.0	25.8	–40.9
Fifth birth	4.1	8.3	4.8	1.8	102.4	–42.2	–62.5	17.1	–56.1
Sixth and seventh births	4.6	7.6	4.5	1.4	65.2	–40.8	–68.9	–2.2	–69.6
Eighth and higher births	3.9	4.3	2.7	0.7	10.3	–37.2	–74.1	–30.8	–82.1
All births (GFR)	91.5	118.0	87.6	66.7	29.0	–25.8	–23.9	–4.3	–27.1

a   Column 5 = $\dfrac{\text{column 2} - \text{column 1}}{\text{column 1}} \times 100$;

Column 6 = $\dfrac{\text{column 3} - \text{column 2}}{\text{column 2}} \times 100$;

Column 7 = $\dfrac{\text{column 4} - \text{column 3}}{\text{column 3}} \times 100$;

Column 8 = $\dfrac{\text{column 3} - \text{column 1}}{\text{column 1}} \times 100$;

Column 9 = $\dfrac{\text{column 4} - \text{column 1}}{\text{column 1}} \times 100$.

Source: U.S. National Center for Health Statistics (1969, Table 1-8; 1978b, Table 1-8).

age-sex adjusted birth rate, which is the crude birth rate standardized for age and sex composition. Because the procedure used in calculating this rate is similar to that used for standardizing the crude death rate, we will not discuss it here. The actual values of age-sex adjusted birth rates, however, are of some interest.

Table 29 presents the crude birth rates and standardized birth rates for 20 countries and dates, based on calculations by Keyfitz and Flieger (1971). The standard populations used are those of England and Wales in 1961, the United States in 1960, and Mexico in 1960. Although many statements can be made about the rates summarized there, we note especially the following two conclusions:

(1) The rank order of countries from highest to lowest birth rate is not affected much by the standardization—that is, the rank-order correlation is high—but a few countries do change in rank when standardized on the age distribution of Mexico in 1960. For example, Réunion has the fourth highest unstandardized rate. Standardized on the 1961 England and Wales and 1960 U.S. age distributions, it retains this ranking. Standardized on the 1960 Mexican age distribution, however, Réunion has a rank of 8.

(2) Even though the rank order of countries is not critically affected by standardization, the amounts of the differences do change substantially. For example, the crude rates are 54.5 for Togo in 1961 and 44.0 for Mexico in 1966. Standardized on the age distribution of Mexico in 1960, the rates are 50.4 for Togo and 46.1 for Mexico. Hence, 59 percent of the difference in crude rates between Mexico and Togo is due to differences in age distribution:

$$\frac{10.5 - 4.3}{10.5} \times 100 = 59.$$

Data for the United States between 1940 and 1975 provide an additional illustration of the use of age-sex adjusted birth rates (Table 30). The crude birth rate in the United States increased from 19.4 in 1940 to a peak of 25.0 in 1955, then declined to 14.8 in 1975. The highest crude birth rates were recorded in the "baby boom" period of the 1950s, right after the Second World War. Although the crude rates of that period were high, they were not nearly as high as they would have been if the age and sex composition of the 1940s had still held in the 1950s. For example, if the age and sex composition of the 1955 population had been the same as the 1940

Table 29. Crude birth rates and directly standardized birth rates, for selected countries and dates

Country	Year or period	Crude birth rate	Crude birth rate standardized using as standard:					
			England and Wales, 1961		United States, 1960		Mexico, 1960	
			Rate	Rank	Rate	Rank	Rate	Rank
Togo	1961	54.5	45.6	1	46.3	1	50.4	1
Madagascar	1966	45.8	43.8	2	44.5	2	48.2	3
El Salvador	1961	49.4	43.3	3	44.1	3	48.9	2
Réunion	1963	44.4	43.0	4	43.7	4	45.8	8
Honduras	1966	44.2	43.0	5	43.7	5	46.9	4
Mexico	1966	44.0	42.4	6	43.1	6	46.1	6
Costa Rica	1966	41.8	41.7	7	42.4	7	46.1	7
Venezuela	1965	43.5	41.1	8	41.8	8	46.6	5
Ceylon	1963	34.6	32.1	9	32.7	9	35.5	9
Thailand	1960	36.5	32.0	10	33.8	10	33.6	11
China (Taiwan)	1965	32.7	30.6	11	31.1	11	35.2	10
Sweden	1778–82	34.5	29.5	12	29.9	12	28.6	13
England and Wales	1861	34.6	29.2	13	29.7	13	30.1	12
Chile	1967	28.4	25.1	14	25.5	14	28.3	14
Portugal	1966–68	21.4	18.5	15	18.8	15	20.5	16
United States	1966	18.4	17.4	16	17.8	16	21.5	15
England and Wales	1967	17.2	16.7	17	17.0	17	20.2	17
Italy	1966	18.4	16.1	18	16.4	18	18.4	18
Sweden	1967	15.4	14.5	19	14.8	19	17.6	19
Japan	1966	13.8	10.0	20	10.1	20	12.0	20

Source: Keyfitz and Flieger (1971:313–487).

Table 30. Crude birth rates and directly standardized birth rates: United States, selected years, 1940—75

Year	Crude birth rate	Age-sex adjusted birth rate using 1940 U.S. age and sex distribution as standard population
1940	19.4	19.4
1945	20.4	20.9
1950	24.1	26.3
1955	25.0	30.4
1960	23.7	31.2
1965	19.4	25.0
1970	18.4	21.3
1975	14.8	15.5

Source: U.S. National Center for Health Statistics (1978b, Tables 1-2 and 1-3).

composition, the birth rate for 1955 would have been 30.5 instead of the observed value of 25.0. In fact, the standardized birth rate for every year after 1940 is higher than the crude rate when the 1940 composition is used as the standard population. The age and sex structure of the United States since 1940 has been less favorable to high crude birth rates than was the 1940 age and sex structure.

It is also possible to standardize more refined fertility measures such as the general fertility rate or even age-specific fertility rates. We have done such calculations in age-standardizing the general fertility rates for Sweden, India, the Philippines, Ireland, and the United States using three standard populations: Sweden in 1970, India in 1971, and the Republic of Korea in 1972. The computation procedure is illustrated in Table 31, which shows the calculations using the Swedish population as standard. The comparable calculations for the India standard and the Korea standard are not shown, but the observed rates and the standardized values are summarized in Table 32. The rank order of the general fertility rates is the same for the actual rates and each set of standardized rates: India has the highest rate and Sweden the lowest, with the Philippines second highest, Ireland third, and the United States fourth. The amounts of the differences, however, are affected by the standards. To take just one example, the ratio of the actual GFR for India to that of Sweden is 3.3 (194.1/59.5). Standardized on the age distribution of Sweden, however, the ratio falls to 2.9 (170.8/59.5). Thus, the age distribution

Table 31. General fertility rates for selected countries, age-
(Standard = Sweden, 1970)

Ages	Standard million for 1970 Sweden females, 15—49 (1)	Age-specific fertility rates, by		
		India (2)	Sweden (3)	Philippines (4)
15—19	139,005	141	34	65
20—24	143,935	313	121	244
25—29	164,581	203	127	301
30—34	175,640	195	69	235
35—39	134,012	179	27	163
40—44	118,309	104	6	76
45—49	124,518	18	0	17
All ages	1,000,000			
General fertility rates (per 1,000)				

a   Rates based on most recent available census data (1970—71 census round).
Sources: Palmore (1978, Table 4); United Nations Statistical Office, Department of
   Center for Health Statistics (1978b, Table 1-6).

of Indian women of ages 15—49 contributes to the high GFR of that country. Of the difference between the actual GFRs (194.1 − 59.5 = 134.6), 17 percent [(23.3/134.6) × 100] was due to differences in age structure between the two countries.

Sixth Set of Multiple-Choice Questions

1. In two countries, *A* and *B*, the age-specific fertility rates per 1,000 are as follows:

Ages	Country *A*	Country *B*
15—24 years	50	50
25—34 years	100	100
35—44 years	60	60

In country *A*, 60 percent of the population is female and 30 percent of the females are between the ages of 15 and 44. In country *B*, 50 percent of the population is female and 35 percent of the females are between the ages of 15 and 44. Assume births occur only to women between the ages of 15 and 44.

(a)   The crude birth rate is higher in country *A* than in country *B*.

standardized by the direct method: recent years

country[a]		Expected number of births				
Ireland (5)	United States (6)	India (1)×(2)	Sweden (1)×(3)	Philip-pines (1)×(4)	Ireland (1)×(5)	United States (1)×(6)
19	68	19,600	4,726	9,035	2,641	9,452
150	168	45,052	17,416	35,120	21,590	24,181
244	145	33,410	20,902	49,539	40,158	23,864
200	73	34,250	12,119	41,275	35,128	12,822
132	32	23,988	3,618	21,844	17,690	4,288
47	8	12,304	710	8,991	5,561	946
3	0	2,241	0	2,117	374	0
		170,845	59,491	167,921	123,142	75,553
		170.84	59.49	167.92	123.14	75.55

Economic and Social Affairs, 1973 *Demographic Yearbook* (1975, Table 7); U.S. National

   (b)   The crude birth rate is lower in country A than in country B.
   (c)   The crude birth rate is equal in the two countries.
   (d)   Any of the above may be true.
2. Using the data in question 1, it is possible to say with certainty that:
   (a)   The general fertility rate is higher in country A than in country B.
   (b)   The general fertility rate is higher in country B than in country A.
   (c)   The general fertility rate is equal in the two countries.
   (d)   Any of the above may be true.
3. Using the data in question 1, it is possible to say with certainty that:
   (a)   The age-sex adjusted birth rate is higher in country A than in country B.
   (b)   The age-sex adjusted birth rate is higher in country B than in country A.
   (c)   The age-sex adjusted birth rates in the two countries are equal.
   (d)   Any of the above may be true.

Table 32. Observed general fertility rates and age-standardized
general fertility rates with Sweden (1970), India (1971),
and Republic of Korea (1972) as standard populations:
India, Sweden, Philippines, Ireland, United States

| Country | GFR | Age-standardized GFR using as standard population: | | |
		Sweden, 1970	India, 1971	Korea, 1972
Sweden	59.5	59.5	63.4	61.0
United States	76.2	75.6	82.4	80.7
Ireland	113.2	123.1	123.1	116.3
Philippines	167.9	167.9	171.3	164.1
India	194.1	170.8	194.1	177.4

Note: GFRs calculated by using the country's age distribution around 1970 (from U.N.
Demographic Yearbooks) and the ASFRs from Table 31. Age-standardized GFRs use
standard age distribution of the country listed and the same ASFRs.

4. As compared with developing nations, the age structures of the
   developed nations tend to be unusually favorable to:
   (a) high crude birth rates and high crude death rates.
   (b) low crude birth rates and high crude death rates.
   (c) low crude birth rates and low crude death rates.
   (d) high crude birth rates and low crude death rates.
   (e) none of the above.

Fifth Set of True-False Questions

Determine whether each of the following statements is true or false.

1. The standardization of crude birth rates makes relatively little difference in the rank order of countries for values of the birth rate,
   but it does affect the sizes of rates relative to one another.
2. It would be possible to construct an age-standardized rate of
   natural increase.
3. Fertility rates specific for live birth order can be constructed only
   as period rates and not as cohort rates.
4. It is possible to standardize means, percentages, proportions, and
   ratios as well as rates.

The Total Fertility Rate

It is now clear that the standardization technique is quite general, and we could apply it to many refined uses—such as the computation of age- and marital status-specific fertility rates standardized on the educational composition of a standard population. Instead, we now turn to a discussion of the total fertility rate (TFR), which is a standardized rate whose values are particularly useful in interpreting the cumulative fertility implied by a given set of age-specific fertility rates.

The *total fertility rate* is defined as the sum of the age-specific fertility rates for women, when age is given in single years. We would usually perform the following calculation to get the total fertility rate:

$$TFR = [\text{ sum of the age-specific fertility rates }] \times 1,000$$

$$= \sum_{x} (F_x) \times 1,000$$

where   TFR = total fertility rate,

$\sum_{x}$ means one should add up the age-specific rates, and

F_x = the age-specific rate for the age group $x, x + 1$.

The total fertility rate is a standardized measure because the age-specific fertility rate at each age is multiplied by a standard population, usually of 1,000 persons, as above. In other words, the total fertility rate assumes a "rectangular" age distribution for the standard population with the same number of persons at each year of age, namely 1,000.[4] In practice, it is usual to sum rates for five-year age groups and to assume that the age-specific rates for each single year are accurately summarized by the average rate for the five-year age group. The formula then becomes $TFR = 5[\sum_{x} {}_5F_x(1,000)]$ (see Table 33).

The TFR is only one type of standardized rate, but its use has been particularly widespread because it has a useful interpretation. The total fertility rate summarizes a *hypothetical* fertility history analogous to the hypothetical mortality history of a cross-sectional life table. It estimates the total number of live births 1,000 women would have if they all lived through their entire reproductive period and were subject to a given set of age-specific fertility rates. In other words, the total fertility rate reports the average number of live

---

4 The total fertility rate may be expressed either per woman or per 1,000 women. In this *Guide*, we express the rate per 1,000 women.

Table 33. Calculation of total fertility rates for the United States: 1957, 1967, and 1975

Ages of women	Age-specific fertility rates per 1,000 women for:		
	1957	1967	1975
10–14	1.0	0.9	1.3
15–19	96.3	67.9	56.3
20–24	260.6	174.0	114.7
25–29	199.4	142.6	110.3
30–34	118.9	79.3	53.1
35–39	59.9	38.5	19.4
40–44	16.3	10.6	4.6
45–49	1.1	0.7	0.3
Sum	753.5	514.5	360.0
Sum × 5 = total fertility rate (per 1,000 women)	3,767.5	2,572.5	1,800.0

Source: U.S. National Center for Health Statistics (1978b, Table 1-6).

births among 1,000 women exposed throughout their childbearing years to the schedule of age-specific fertility rates currently in effect, assuming no woman died during the childbearing years.

Actually, age-specific fertility rates change from year to year, and it is not likely that the age-specific rates for a specific calendar year would remain the same throughout the reproductive years of a woman. Just as do measures from a cross-sectional life table, the total fertility rate reflects what would happen to a hypothetical or "synthetic" cohort of women. The rate can only be interpreted to reflect completed family size when we assume that the age-specific fertility rates for women 20–24 years old now will still be the same when women 15–19 become 20–24 in five years' time, and when we also make similar assumptions for the other age groups.

In the early 1970s, total fertility rates as high as 7,705 (Kenya) and as low as 1,841 (German Democratic Republic) were estimated (Palmore, 1978). The higher total fertility rates are found in the developing areas just as are higher crude birth rates and higher general fertility rates. In fact, all the common measures of fertility we have discussed thus far are highly correlated with one another, at least at this historical juncture. Using the fertility measures for 50 nations with reliable data for the 1955—60 period, Bogue and Palmore (1964) reported the following correlations:

(a) .992 between the crude birth rate and the general fertility rate,

(b) .980 between the crude birth rate and the general fertility rate standardized on the estimated age composition of the world, and

(c) .982 between the crude birth rate and the total fertility rate.

These three correlation coefficients summarize only a few of the relationships, but coefficients above .979 were found between all the fertility rates we have presented to this point except for the various age-specific rates. The age pattern of fertility is more variable within a specific overall fertility level, but even the lowest correlations were still quite high and can be illustrated by the following two values: The lowest correlation between the total fertility rate and an age-specific rate was .711 and the lowest correlation between the standardized GFR and an age-specific rate was .689. Even the correlations between age-specific rates without controlling for the overall fertility level were .425 or greater.

Since the various measures of fertility are so highly correlated, you may well ask why there are so many. Why don't scholars use just one? There are several reasons:

(a) The data necessary for calculating any given measure may not be available. For example, for a certain country one may be able to compute only the crude birth rate because data on the age and sex distribution or on live births by age of mother are not available.

(b) We cannot be certain that the high correlations of the 1955—60 period have always obtained in the past, and they may not obtain in the future. Rapid changes in fertility are occurring in some countries, and the age distribution depends on fertility. Hence, we may get different results in the future. In their article on Hong Kong, Freedman and Adlakha (1968) illustrate the types of changes that can occur and how the different measures help our understanding of what has been happening there.

(c) The values of different measures are highly correlated, but the values for specific countries may be deviant. It may not be wise to assume that because country *A* has a higher crude birth rate than country *B,* the total fertility rate in country *A* is also higher than in country *B.* Further, even if the direction of the difference in two rates is the same with different measures, the amount of the difference between the fertility rates of two populations may be different, depending on which measure is used.

(d)   Finally, an important reason for having a variety of measures is that each measure answers a somewhat different question about the fertility level.

To cite an example of the last point using the rate we have most recently discussed, we can interpret the total fertility rate in a way that is not possible with either the crude birth rate or the general fertility rate. Whereas the total fertility rate summarizes the data for the same group of women as the general fertility rate, for example, the TFR takes into account the distribution of births within the child-bearing years and uses the same standard population in every calculation. It is this feature that allows the completed family size interpretation of the TFR for a hypothetical cohort of women.

Gross and Net Reproduction Rates

Other measures give us yet additional information about the reproductive behavior of a population. One meaningful question, for example, is whether a given set of fertility rates implies that the population will grow, exactly replace itself, or decline. In a way, this is more a question about natural increase than about fertility itself. The gross and net reproduction rates are often used to provide partial answers to this type of question.

The *gross reproduction rate* (GRR) is a standardized rate similar to the total fertility rate except that it is the sum of age-specific rates that include only female live births in the numerators.[5] The formula for the calculation is as follows:

$$GRR = (5 \text{ times the sum of five-year age-specific fertility rates including only female births}) \times 1,000$$

$$= 5 \sum_x {}_5 F_x^f (1,000)$$

---

5   No firm standard has been established on whether to express the gross reproduction rate per woman or per 1,000 women. In this *Guide,* we express it per 1,000 women to maintain consistency with the age-specific rates, the crude rate, and the general fertility rate. It is probably somewhat more common to express the rate per woman.

where GRR = gross reproduction rate,

$\sum\limits_{x}$ means one should sum the age-specific rates, and

$_5F_x^f$ = the number of female live births to women of age group x, $x+5$ divided by the midyear population of women in age group x, $x+5$.

Since the number of female live births by age of mother may not be known, the proportion of all births that are female is often used as a constant multiplier for the age-specific rates to obtain the data required for the gross reproduction rate. An example of the calculation of the gross reproduction rate using this method is given in Table 34.

Note that in the above formula, we multiply the sum of the ASFRs by 5, because we are dealing with five-year rates; each woman in the hypothetical cohort of ages 20–24 will experience $_5F_{20}^f$ for five years. This amounts to the same thing as summing the single-year ASFRs, as we did when calculating the TFR, above.

Like the total fertility rate, the gross reproduction rate, when multiplied by 1,000, can be interpreted as the number of daughters expected to be born alive to a hypothetical cohort of 1,000 women

Table 34. Calculation of the gross reproduction rate for Costa Rica: 1960

Ages of women	Age-specific fertility rates (per 1,000 women)	ASFRs × proportion of births female (0.4916)
15–19	138.7	68.2
20–24	389.7	191.6
25–29	378.3	186.0
30–34	310.0	152.4
35–39	246.6	121.2
40–44	102.5	50.4
45–49	17.4	8.6
Sum		778.4
Sum × 5 = gross reproduction rate (per 1,000 women)		3,892.0

Note: As is often done, the few births to women less than 15 years old are attributed to women of ages 15–19. Although not necessary here, this is also often done for births to women over 49, attributing them to women 45–49.

Source of data: Keyfitz and Flieger (1968:94).

if no women died during the childbearing years and if the same
schedule of age-specific rates applied throughout the childbearing
years. The advantage of using only female births in the calculations is
that the GRR then measures the extent to which a hypothetical cohort of women will replace itself, provided no woman dies in the
childbearing years.

In the 1970s, values of the gross reproduction rate (expressed per
1,000 women) were as high as 3,290 (non-Jewish population of
Israel, 1975–77) and as low as 670 (Federal Republic of Germany,
1978), according to the Office of Population Research (1981: pp.
402–11). Around 1970, the average GRR for the developing regions
was between 2,700 and 3,500, while the average for the developed
regions was about 1,000 (see Table 35). Whereas 92 percent of the
more developed regions had gross reproduction rates of 1,500 or less,
94 percent of the developing regions had GRRs of more than 1,500
and 84 percent had rates higher than 2,300 (see Table 36).

Of course, the gross reproduction rate measures only fertility,
without any allowance for the fact that some women may die during
the childbearing years. To get a more accurate measure of the replacement of women by their daughters in the hypothetical cohort, we
must use the net reproduction rate.

The *net reproduction rate* (NRR) when multiplied by 1,000 is a
measure of the number of daughters that will be born to a hypothetical cohort of 1,000 women, taking into account the mortality of the
1,000 women from the time of their birth.[6] Hence, the net reproduction rate estimates the average number of daughters who will replace
a cohort of 1,000 female infants by the time the cohort has been sub-
jected to the risk of mortality from ages 0 to 49 and the risks of live
birth from ages 15 to 49. We start with a hypothetical cohort of
1,000 girls just born. Only a certain proportion of these 1,000 girls
will live to reach the childbearing period. Further, within the childbearing period mortality will also take its toll, so that a given woman
might bear daughters through age 30, say, but not live to age 50. The
net reproduction rate is designed to provide an estimate of replacement in the hypothetical cohort, given mortality levels taken from a
current life table.

The computational procedures for the net reproduction rate are
illustrated in Table 37. We first enter the age-specific fertility rates

---

6 Like the GRR, the NRR may be expressed per woman or per 1,000 women.

Table 35. **Estimated crude birth rates and gross reproduction rates**
for world regions: around 1970

Region	Crude birth rates	Gross reproduction rates
All regions	**29.8**	**2,200**
Less developed regions	**34.6**	**2,500**
More developed regions	**15.4**	**1,000**
Africa	**46.9**	**3,200**
North Africa	43.4	3,100
Southern Africa	43.1	2,900
East Africa	48.0	3,300
West Africa	49.6	3,300
Middle Africa	44.7	2,800
Asia (excluding U.S.S.R.)	**32.5**	**2,400**
Southwest Asia	47.0	3,500
South Central Asia	37.5	2,900
Southeast Asia	41.5	2,800
East Asia	25.3	1,700
Middle and South America	**34.5**	**2,400**
Middle America	38.5	2,800
South America	31.3	2,100
North America	**15.3**	**800**
Europe	**13.8**	**1,000**
Northern Europe	12.3	1,000
Southern Europe	16.2	1,200
Eastern Europe	16.5	1,100
Western Europe	10.5	700
Oceania	**18.4**	**1,200**
U.S.S.R.	**18.2**	**1,200**

Note: Provisional weighted averages of most recent available rates for countries within each region. Original sources give gross reproduction rates per woman. All GRR entries here were multiplied by 1,000.

Sources: United Nations (1980, Tables 7 and 8); United Nations Statistical Office, Department of Economic and Social Affairs, 1975 *Demographic Yearbook* (1976, Tables 5 and 22).

including only female live births (column 3 of Table 37). Next, we enter the values for the number of person-years lived in each age interval, using the $_5L_x$ column from an abridged life table for females in the current period (column 4). Since the rates in column 3 are expressed per 1,000 women, we express the $_5L_x$ values per woman so

Table 36. Distribution of world regions, by level of gross reproduction rate: 1965–75

Level of gross reproduction rate	All regions	Less developed regions	More developed regions	Africa	Asia (excluding U.S.S.R.)	South America	Europe (excluding U.S.S.R.)	North America	Oceania	U.S.S.R.
Total	117	83	34	34	30	10	25	14	3	1
Under 900	5	0	5	0	0	0	5	0	0	0
900–1,299	22	1	21	0	2	0	15	2	2	1
1,300–1,599	7	2	5	0	1	2	3	1	0	0
1,600–1,999	7	5	2	0	3	1	1	2	0	0
2,000–2,399	4	3	1	0	2	0	1	1	0	0
2,400–2,699	7	7	0	2	1	2	0	2	0	0
2,700–2,999	17	17	0	8	5	2	0	1	1	0
3,000–3,299	22	22	0	10	7	3	0	2	0	0
3,300–3,599	26	26	0	14	9	0	0	3	0	0
3,600+	0	0	0	0	0	0	0	0	0	0

Note: Countries with populations under 1 million are excluded. Countries with unreliable data excluded except in cases where reliable estimates have been made. More developed countries and regions include Australia, Canada, Europe, Japan, New Zealand, Temperate South America, the United States, and the U.S.S.R.

Source: United Nations Statistical Office, Department of Economic and Social Affairs, 1975 *Demographic Yearbook* (1976, Table 22).

Table 37. **Calculation of the gross and net reproduction rates and the length of a generation for the United States, 1975 nonwhite population**

Ages (1)	Midpoint of age interval (2)	Female births per 1,000 women per year[a] (3)	Person-years lived in age interval (per female) = $_5L_x/100,000$ (4)	Female births per 1,000 women for 5-year period = Col. (4) × Col. (3) (5)	Col. (5) × Col. (2) (6)
10–14	12.5	.23	4.85882	1.12	14.000
15–19	17.5	53.31	4.84739	258.41	4,522.175
20–24	22.5	70.43	4.82586	339.89	7,647.525
25–29	27.5	55.11	4.79553	264.28	7,267.700
30–34	32.5	29.75	4.75722	141.53	4,599.725
35–39	37.5	13.61	4.70205	63.99	2,399.625
40–44	42.5	3.87	4.61839	17.87	759.475
45–49	47.5	.25	4.49498	1.12	53.200
Sum	na	226.56	na	1,088.21	27,263.425

Note: Gross reproduction rate = sum of col. (3) × 5 = 1,132.80. Net reproduction rate = sum of col. (5) = 1,088.21. Length of a generation = 27,263.425/1,088.21 = 25.05 years.

na–not applicable.

a   Calculated by multiplying the proportion female of births in each five-year age group by the age-specific fertility rate for that age group.

Sources: U.S. National Center for Health Statistics (1978b, Tables 1-6 and 1-52; 1978c, Table 5-1).

that we do not multiply by 1,000 twice. We then take the product of the $_5L_x$ values and the age-specific rates (column 3 multiplied by column 4). The $_5L_x$ values refer to a five-year period, and therefore we do not need to multiply by 5 to get the NRR as we do with the GRR; the NRR is simply the sum of the products of columns 3 and 4, or 1,088.21 per 1,000 in the present example.

Expressed in a formula, the calculation of the net reproduction rate is as follows:

NRR = the sum of the multiplications of (a) each five-year age-specific fertility rate including only female live births and (b) the number of person-years lived in the stationary population for the age interval corresponding to the fertility rate

$$= \sum_x (_5F_x^f) \left(\frac{_5L_x}{\ell_0} \right)$$

where NRR = net reproduction rate,

$\sum_x$ means one should sum the products for every age group,

$_sF_x^f$ = the age-specific fertility rates (per 1,000 women[7]) including only female live births in the numerator, and

$(_sL_x/\ell_0)$ = the number of person-years lived (per 1 woman) in the age interval, and x refers to the exact age at the beginning of the age interval.

Rates as high as 3,127 (non-Jewish population of Israel, 1975–77) per 1,000 women and as low as 650 (Federal Republic of Germany, 1978) per 1,000 women have been cited for countries in the 1970s (Office of Population Research, 1981: pp. 402–11). Of course, it is difficult to interpret the precise meaning of these net rates unless we compare them with the gross reproduction rates. A country may have a low net reproduction rate because fertility rates are low, because mortality rates are high, or both. To take two examples from a single country, Japan in 1930–34 had a GRR of 2,320 and an NRR of 1,620 per 1,000 women (Table 38).[8] With these data, we would say that fertility was moderately high and mortality was high. By 1977, however, Japan had a gross reproduction rate of 870 and a net reproduction rate of 860 per 1,000 women. Both fertility and mortality rates were low. The reader may find it useful to interpret other figures in Tables 38, 39, and 40 or to refer to a more complete listing such as that given in Keyfitz and Flieger (1971).

We can interpret the net reproduction rate as a measure of how many daughters would replace 1,000 women if age-specific fertility and mortality rates remained constant for a sufficient length of time. Consequently, rates above 1,000 mean that eventually the population would increase and rates below 1,000 mean that eventually the population would decrease, provided that the age-specific rates remained the same and no migration occurred. Rates like 3,127 imply a speedy rate of increase if age-specific rates do not change.

---

7 Using fertility rates per 1,000 women is equivalent to multiplying their sum by 1,000, as we did above for the TFR and the GRR.

8 Note that in Table 38, intrinsic rates, such as the GRR and NRR, refer to what would happen if ASFRs and ASDRs were to continue indefinitely into the future.

The Mean Length of a Generation

Another measure of replacement that follows easily from the calculations performed for the net reproduction rate is the mean length of a
generation. This measure answers the question: On the average, how
many years after birth does a woman replace herself with female
children? The measure is designed to give an indication of the speed
with which each woman replaces herself with potential mothers.

The length of a generation is a weighted sum of the female births
per 1,000 women for each five-year period, all divided by the net
reproduction rate—that is, it is the average age of women at the birth
of their children. The weights used are the ages of the women. The
calculation is illustrated by the computations in Table 37 for the
U.S. nonwhite population in 1975. We get the mean length of a generation by multiplying the midpoints of each age interval (column 2)
by the female births per 1,000 women for the five-year period (column 5) and then dividing the result by the net reproduction rate (the
sum of column 5).

From the calculation procedure, it is clear that the length of the
generation is affected by two things, the overall fertility and mortality levels and the proportionate distribution of fertility into each
age-specific rate. This is true because every age-specific female birth
rate would be affected by the overall fertility and mortality level
(i.e., columns 4 and 3 would have lower entries in general if the overall level of fertility were lower and mortality were higher) and because higher age-specific fertility rates at the younger ages would lead
to a lower value of the mean length of the generation.

In recent years, values of the mean length of a generation have
varied between less than 25 years (Bulgaria) and almost 30 years
(Ireland) in countries for which the data required to calculate the
measure are available (Office of Population Research, 1981: pp. 402–
11). This means that, barring changes in age-specific fertility and mortality rates and assuming no migration, the average woman, living in
countries with the necessary data to allow calculation of the mean
length of a generation, will replace herself with daughters in no
fewer than 25 and no more than 30 years.

The length of a generation is important, because it affects the rate
of growth of a population independently of the number of children
born as measured by the net reproduction rate. This is so because the
more rapidly a generation replaces itself, the more rapidly it will add

Table 38. Selected illustrative reproduction measures, comparing intrinsic and crude rates

| Country and date | Gross reproduction rate | Net reproduction rate | Mean age at childbirth | Life expectancy at birth | Vital rates (female population) | | | | |
| | | | | | Intrinsic rates | | | Crude rates | |
					Natural increase	Births	Deaths	Births	Deaths
Canada									
1930–34	1,480	1,280	30.0	62.5	8.3	21.3	13.0	22.9	10.0
1950–54	1,760	1,670	28.4	71.3	18.4	26.0	7.6	27.5	7.5
1977	880	860	26.8	77.5	-5.5	10.3	15.8	15.0	6.0
1978	860	840	26.9	77.5	-6.3	9.9	16.3	u	u
China (Taiwan)									
1955–59	3,010	2,670	30.3	65.0	33.3	40.7	7.4	42.8	7.6
1965–69	2,150	2,020	28.1	69.9	25.5	32.1	6.6	30.0	4.8
1978	1,310	1,260	26.3	73.5	8.9	18.8	9.9	24.5	3.9
1979	1,280	1,240	26.2	73.0	8.2	18.5	10.3	24.6	3.9
Costa Rica									
1960–64	3,440	2,950	29.7	64.2	37.5	46.1	8.6	47.9	7.8
1975	1,880	1,750	27.8	73.5	20.5	27.6	7.1	28.5	4.2
Denmark									
1930–34	1,060	940	29.4	63.6	-2.5	14.3	16.9	17.2	10.9
1946–49	1,260	1,280	28.4	70.0	8.7	19.5	10.8	20.3	9.1
1978	810	800	26.6	77.5	-8.4	9.0	17.4	11.7	9.4
1979	780	770	26.7	77.4	-9.7	8.5	18.2	11.2	9.6
France									
1930–34	1,080	910	28.2	59.8	-3.8	14.6	18.2	16.4	14.8
1946–47	1,460	1,330	29.1	67.0	9.9	21.1	11.2	19.7	12.6
1976	890	880	27.1	77.2	-4.7	10.4	15.4	13.0	9.9
1978	900	880	27.1	78.0	-4.5	10.6	15.2	13.2	9.6

Hungary									
1930–31	1,390	1,040	27.0	51.8	1.3	20.3	19.0	23.3	15.2
1952–54	1,320	1,200	27.0	67.1	6.7	19.0	12.3	20.0	10.7
1977	1,060	1,010	24.9	72.4	0.2	14.0	13.8	15.8	11.5
1978	1,010	970	24.8	73.3	−1.3	13.0	14.3	14.9	12.2
Japan									
1930–34	2,320	1,620	30.4	48.2	16.3	33.8	17.4	u	u
1955–59	1,040	960	28.6	68.6	−1.3	13.9	15.2	17.3	7.2
1977	870	860	27.5	77.4	−5.5	10.3	15.8	14.8	5.5
Netherlands									
1930–34	1,370	1,230	31.2	65.9	6.6	19.2	12.6	20.5	8.7
1960–64	1,550	1,510	29.5	75.9	14.2	21.9	7.7	20.2	7.0
1977	770	770	27.5	78.4	−9.6	8.4	18.0	12.1	7.0
1978	770	760	27.5	78.5	−9.6	8.4	18.0	12.2	7.2
Romania									
1956	1,410	1,260	27.7	65.0	8.2	20.6	12.4	23.0	9.6
1962–64	950	890	26.2	70.0	−4.6	12.0	16.6	14.9	8.3
1978	1,230	1,170	25.6	72.2	6.2	17.5	11.2	18.2	9.1
1979	1,210	1,150	25.5	72.2	5.6	17.1	11.5	17.8	9.3
United States									
1935–39	1,090	960	27.5	63.5	−1.8	14.8	16.6	18.4	9.9
1955–59	1,800	1,730	26.4	72.8	21.1	27.7	6.6	23.9	8.0
1977	890	880	25.9	77.1	−5.2	10.5	15.7	14.6	7.7
1978	880	860	26.0	77.2	−5.7	10.3	15.9	14.5	7.8

u–data unavailable.

Source: Office of Population Research (1980a:352–60; 1981:402–11). Source lists gross reproduction rates and net reproduction rates per woman. Here they are per 1,000 women.

Fertility

Table 39. Gross and net reproduction rates for Europe: depression
years, post World War II, and recent past

Region and country	Early 1930s		Middle 1960s		Late 1970s		Date
	GRR	NRR	GRR	NRR	GRR	NRR	
Northwestern and Western Europe							
Austria	890	740	1,300	1,240	790	770	(1979)
Denmark	1,040	920	1,270	1,240	780	770	(1979)
England and Wales	930	810	1,330	1,290	850	830	(1978)
France	1,100	920	1,350	1,320	900	880	(1978)
Germany[a]	800	720	1,220	1,170	670	650	(1978)
Netherlands	1,310	1,190	1,480	1,430	770	760	(1978)
Norway	1,040	960	1,410	1,370	850	840	(1979)
Sweden	820	730	1,150	1,130	810	800	(1979)
Southern and Eastern Europe							
Greece	1,870	1,250	1,090	1,000	1,100	1,030	(1977)
Hungary	1,390	1,040	910	860	1,010	970	(1978)
Italy	1,580	1,220	1,300	1,220	940	910	(1977)
Poland	1,710	1,240	1,220	1,150	1,080	1,050	(1977)
Portugal	1,870	1,290	1,520	1,350	1,260	1,160	(1975)
Yugoslavia	2,200	1,390	1,280	1,150	1,050	1,000	(1977)

a   Federal Republic of Germany after World War II.

Sources: Office of Population Research (1950:172–78; 1968:249–54; 1981:402–11).
Sources list gross reproduction rates and net reproduction rates per woman. Here they
are given per 1,000 women.

new members to the population (at whatever rate *per generation*
prevails). The net reproduction rate tells us how much a population
is growing per generation. It does not tell us how long the generation
is.

The United States has a rather short generation length compared
with Western Europe, because average age at marriage and childbearing is younger in the U.S., as shown in Tables 38–40. Therefore,
even if U.S. families were no larger than those of Europe, the U.S.
population growth rate would be greater, because the cycle of reproduction is repeated more rapidly. For these reasons, the age pattern
of fertility decline in countries with high fertility is important. If the
net reproduction rate falls by 10 percent as a result of changes in fertility among older women, it will have less effect than an equal

Table 40. Gross and net reproduction rates, by color: United States, 1905—77

Year	Gross reproduction rate			Net reproduction rate		
	Total	White	Non-white	Total	White	Non-white
1905—10	1,790	1,740	2,240	1,340	1,340	1,330
1930—35	1,110	1,080	1,340	980	970	1,070
1935—40	1,100	1,060	1,410	980	960	1,140
1946—49	1,510	1,480	1,780	1,420	1,400	1,540
1950—54	1,630	1,560	2,070	1,550	1,500	1,840
1955—59	1,800	1,730	2,330	1,730	1,670	2,110
1960—64	1,690	1,620	2,160	1,620	1,570	1,980
1965—69	1,280	1,220	1,700	1,240	1,190	1,570
1970—74	1,030	980	1,330	1,000	960	1,250
1975	880	830	1,140	860	820	1,100
1976	850	820	1,120	850	800	1,080
1977	890	840	1,150	880	830	1,110

Note: Source data are multiplied by 1,000.

Sources: 1905—40: Office of Population Research (1950:172). 1946—77: Office of Population Research (1979:352).

decline among younger women. There are some notable differences in this respect. For example, women in India have their children at early ages (as compared, for example, with Chinese women in Singapore or Malaysia or Taiwan). This means that the growth rate for India is likely to be higher even if the total number of children born per woman is no greater than in the other populations where child-bearing takes place at older ages. Changing the age at which women bear children can, in itself, have an effect on the growth rate.

Exercise 5

Alter the fertility rates in column 3 of Table 37 in such a way as to retain the same sum (i.e., keep the same gross reproduction rate). Do this by increasing the rates for younger women and decreasing the rates for older women. What effect does this have on the net reproduction rate? What effect does this have on the mean length of a generation?

Exercise 6

How would you interpret the following combinations of information for various countries? Assume that there is no net migration affecting the age structure in any of these countries.

Country	Gross reproduction rate	Net reproduction rate	Crude birth rate	Crude death rate
A	1,000	985	14	14
B	1,000	985	17	6
C	3,000	2,950	Not available	Not available
D	3,000	1,000	45	45
E	1,500	1,485	Not available	Not available
F	3,000	1,500	45	22

Sixth Set of True-False Questions

Determine whether each of the following statements is true or false.

1. The net reproduction rate can never be higher than the gross reproduction rate.
2. If the gross reproduction rate falls in any given year, it inevitably means that at least a minority of the women in the childbearing years will end up with fewer children than they would have had prior to the decline.
3. Regardless of which fertility measure we use, we will find that fertility is higher in most of the developing areas of the world than in the developed areas.
4. For all practical purposes, the gross reproduction rate is equal to the product of the total fertility rate times the proportion of live births that are female.
5. A gross reproduction rate of 1,500 is very high.
6. A total fertility rate of 2,350 is very high.
7. For most of human history, it is likely that net reproduction rates close to 1,000 were common.

Seventh Set of Multiple-Choice Questions

1. The net reproduction rate in the United States is now approximately:
   (a) 4,000—5,000 per 1,000 women.
   (b) 500—1,000 per 1,000 women.
   (c) 1,000—1,500 per 1,000 women.

(d)   2,500–3,500 per 1,000 women.

(e)   none of the above.

What is it in your own country?

2. A net reproduction rate of more than 1,000 means that:

(a)   a population will certainly increase in the future.

(b)   a population will certainly decrease in the future.

(c)   a population will eventually increase if age-specific fertility and mortality rates remain fixed and there is no migration.

(d)   a population will eventually decrease if age-specific fertility and mortality rates remain fixed and there is no migration.

(e)   a population will remain at about the same size if age-specific fertility and mortality rates remain fixed and there is no migration.

3. The American Hutterites had a gross reproduction rate of 4,000 and a net reproduction rate of 3,660 during one period. This indicates that:

(a)   both mortality and fertility were very high.

(b)   both mortality and fertility were very low.

(c)   fertility was very high and mortality was moderately low.

(d)   mortality was moderately high and fertility was very low.

(e)   mortality was very low and fertility was only moderately high.

4. The net reproduction rate is a measure of the:

(a)   annual excess of births over deaths.

(b)   annual rate at which women are replacing themselves on the basis of prevailing fertility and mortality, assuming no migration.

(c)   decennial growth rate of the population.

(d)   per generation growth rate assuming current age-specific fertility and mortality and no net migration.

(e)   none of the above.

5. In two countries, *A* and *B,* the age-specific fertility rates per 1,000 women for female births are as follows:

Age group	Country *A*	Country *B*
10–19	25	25
20–29	100	100
30–39	50	50
40–49	25	25

In country *A,* 60 percent of the population is female whereas only 50 percent of the population is female in country *B.* In country *A,* 35 percent of the females are between the ages of 10 and 49, whereas 40 percent of the females in country *B* are between the ages of 10 and 49.
  (a) Country *A* has a higher gross reproduction rate than country *B.*
  (b) Country *B* has a higher gross reproduction rate than country *A.*
  (c) Country *A* has the same gross reproduction rate as country *B.*
  (d) Country *A* has the same net reproduction rate as country *B.*
  (e) The crude birth rates are the same in both countries.
  (f) The general fertility rates are the same in both countries.
  (g) Two of the above are correct.
  (h) Three of the above are correct.
6. Populations with net reproduction rates of 1,000 per 1,000 women:
  (a) invariably have low age-specific fertility rates.
  (b) have low crude birth rates but may have high age-specific fertility rates.
  (c) have declining age-specific fertility rates.
  (d) may have either high or low age-specific fertility rates.
  (e) invariably have low crude birth rates.

Census Measures of Fertility

To this point, we have discussed an interlocking system of measures that usually requires both census data for the denominators and vital statistics measures for the numerators.[9] In many countries, vital registration systems either do not exist or are inaccurate in recording the number of vital events or the characteristics of the persons who gave birth or died (e.g., age, place of residence). In countries where this is true, other measures of fertility have been used as substitutes for the measures we have already discussed. Such census measures have an advantage over vital statistics measures in that they allow a

---

9 Sample survey information is sometimes used to collect both the numerators and denominators, and it is possible for a census to collect the information for both numerator and denominator. It is difficult, however, to obtain accurate reporting on births in a census, given the levels of training and supervision normally employed.

much more thorough study of differential fertility, since censuses collect much more information than do birth certificates on many characteristics of individuals—such as income, education, rural-urban residence—which are important because of their effects on fertility.

Most of the major nations of the world have had at least one census in the last ten years, and these data can be used to calculate various indirect measures of fertility. The most common indirect measures are the following:

(1) ratio of children 0—4 years old to women of ages 15—49 or 15—44 years,
(2) ratio of children 5—9 years old to women of ages 15—49 or 15—44 years,
(3) percentage of the total population 0—4 years old,
(4) percentage of the total population 5—9 years old,
(5) percentage of the total population 0—14 years old,
(6) number of children ever born to women, by five-year age groups of the women, and
(7) the number of own (as opposed to adopted) children under age five for women, by five-year age groups of women.

We discuss only the first and sixth measures here, because the problems in interpretation and use are similar for the first five and the last two measures.

The ratio of children 0—4 years old to women of ages 15—44 or 15—49 is often called the *child-woman ratio* (CWR). It can be expressed algebraically as follows:

$$\text{CWR} = k \; \frac{_5P_0}{_{35}P_{15}^f} \quad \text{or} \quad k \; \frac{_5P_0}{_{30}P_{15}^f}$$

where $_5P_0$ = population 0—4 years old,

$_{35}P_{15}^f$ = number of women 15—49 years old, and

$k = 1{,}000.$

The child-woman ratio is based not on births, but on the survivors of births occurring during the last five years. The deaths of children in those five years are not accounted for, and, although the deaths of women in the childbearing years partly compensate for the deaths to children, the net result is that the ratio underestimates fertility. A further problem caused by the fact that the ratio deals with survivors is that two populations may have the same fertility rates but the child-woman ratios will not reflect this if one area has higher child mortality rates. The area with the higher death rates will have a lower child-woman ratio.

There are several other problems with using the child-woman ratio. One is that it measures past fertility (on the average, the fertility of 2.5 years before the census date). Another is that young children are more likely than others to be underenumerated in a census. For that reason, the ratio of children 5–9 years old is sometimes used, but this aggravates the problem of measuring current fertility, because the ratio then refers, on the average, to fertility 7.5 years before the census date.

Even with all these problems, of course, any reasonable measure is better than none, and the child-woman ratio has been used repeatedly when vital registration data are lacking for a country or for subdivisions of a country. In the 1970s, the child-woman ratio for most countries was in the range of 313 (Sweden) to 928 (Western Samoa) per 1,000 women (Palmore, 1978), and the ratio was well correlated with more direct measures of fertility in countries with reliable data. Palmore has estimated that the child-woman ratio had the following correlations with direct measures of fertility for 56 nations with reliable data around 1970: .961 with the crude birth rate, .975 with the general fertility rate, and .970 with the total fertility rate. On the basis of this information, he developed a series of equations for determining the level of direct measures of fertility using census measures like the child-woman ratio and other selected facts about the population. The material is beyond the scope of the present *Guide,* but the interested reader may want to refer to those techniques (Palmore, 1978).

Data on *children ever born* (CEB) are collected in fewer censuses than the data required for calculating the child-woman ratio. For measures of this type, the census must contain a question for each woman asking her how many live births she has ever had. This information can then be tabulated by the woman's age, yielding measures of the cumulative fertility of women up to specified points in their childbearing years. Like the child-woman ratio, statistics on children ever born measure past fertility and are subject to the additional problem that children who die young may not be remembered. Nevertheless, this type of data has been used widely, as is illustrated

Table 41. Percentage ever married and number of children ever born for women of ages 45—49 and 30—34: United States, 1940—78

| Ages of women in given year | Percentage ever married | Percentage childless among ever married | Children ever born | |
			Per 1,000 women	Per 1,000 ever married women
45—49				
1978	95	7.2	3,103	3,236
1970	95	10.8	2,707	2,840
1960	93	18.1	2,245	2,402
1950	92	20.4	2,292	2,492
1940	91	16.8	2,740	2,998
30—34				
1978	91	11.6	1,990	2,135
1970	93	8.3	2,640	2,804
1960	93	10.4	2,445	2,627
1950	91	17.3	1,871	2,059
1940	85	23.3	1,678	1,964

Sources: U.S. Bureau of the Census (1966:11, 12; 1979:32—4).

in Tables 41—45. One reason for the wide use of this measures is based on the notion of cohort fertility, a concept we discuss next.

Cohort Fertility Measures

When we discussed the life table in the mortality chapter, we pointed out that there were two types of life table, the period or cross-sectional life table and the generation or longitudinal life table. A similar distinction can be made among fertility measures. Thus far, we have discussed mostly what are known as *period* or *calendar-year* fertility rates. When we discussed the total fertility rate, however, we introduced the idea of a cohort, albeit a hypothetical or synthetic cohort. It is also possible to construct fertility rates for real cohorts, and measures so constructed are called *cohort* fertility measures.

Two types of cohorts commonly discussed in fertility measurement are marriage cohorts and birth cohorts. If we discuss data for a birth cohort, we refer to the fertility rates for a group of women all

Table 42. Number of children ever born per 1,000 women and per 1,000 married women, by age: United States, selected years, 1940–78

Ages	1940	1950	1960	1970	1978
All women					
15–44	1,238	1,395	1,746	1,918[a]	1,583[a]
15–19	68	105	127	206[b]	174[b]
20–24	522	738	1,032	736	556
25–29	1,132	1,436	2,006	1,790	1,250
30–34	1,678	1,871	2,445	2,640	1,990
35–39	2,145	2,061	2,523	3,015	2,673
40–44	2,490	2,170	2,409	2,952	3,096
45–49	2,740	2,292	2,245	2,707	3,103
Ever married women					
15–44	1,904	1,859	2,314	2,357	2,040
15–19	572	604	792	633	548
20–24	987	1,082	1,441	1,064	908
25–29	1,463	1,654	2,241	1,978	1,443
30–34	1,964	2,059	2,627	2,804	2,135
35–39	2,414	2,247	2,686	3,167	2,788
40–44	2,754	2,364	2,564	3,096	3,212
45–49	2,998	2,492	2,402	2,840	3,236

[a] Numbers for ages 18–44.
[b] Numbers for ages 18 and 19.
Sources: U.S. Bureau of the Census (1966:12; 1979:32–3).

born in the same year or group of years. For example, we might talk about the 1935–39 birth cohort of women. If discussing marriage cohorts, we refer to the fertility rates for a group of women all married in the same year or group of years (e.g., women of the 1940–44 marriage cohort). Usually, use of the word "cohort" by itself refers to a birth cohort, and we will devote most of our discussion here to data for birth cohorts of women.

One rationale for using birth cohort fertility measures hinges on the fact that childbearing in a particular year is partly determined by how many children women have had in preceding years; and this, in turn, is partly determined by their age. A further rationale for using birth cohort measures is based on the argument that family-size ideals

Table 43. Number of children ever born to ever married women, by woman's education and color, for women 35–39 years old in 1970, and percentage of women ever married in each educational category, by color: United States

Years of schooling completed	White		Nonwhite	
	Number of children ever born (per 1,000)	Percentage of women[a]	Number of children ever born (per 1,000)	Percentage of women[a]
0	4,147	0.4	4,349	0.6
1–7	3,800	5.4	4,931	13.4
8	3,474	6.1	4,609	9.0
9–11	3,359	20.1	4,299	33.5
12	3,021	47.1	3,326	30.0
13–15	2,944	11.8	2,851	7.3
16+	2,626	9.0	2,125	6.1
All educational levels	3,119	99.9	3,881	99.9

a   Total percentage does not equal 100.0 because of rounding.

Source: U.S. Bureau of the Census (1973, Tables 42 and 43).

in a culture may change over time. Further, other changes in a society may occur that lead to a different pattern of childbearing in successive generations. Examples of such changes are a war that disrupts family formation during one generation and the development of new methods of controlling fertility that were not previously available.

The fertility of a population may be influenced by both cohort effects and period effects. For example, an economic depression might affect many cohorts simultaneously (although at different stages of their reproductive histories), causing a low level of period fertility during the depression. Once the depression passed, period fertility might rise, and women who had postponed having children during the depression might make up for the postponement. Some cohorts, however, would have reached the end of their reproductive years by the time the depression had ended and would no longer be able to bear children. Such a depression-induced fall in fertility is an example of a period effect.

Table 44. Number of children ever born to married women living
with husbands, by husband's occupation in 1969 and by
color, for women 35–39 years old in 1970, and
percentage of husbands in each occupational category:
United States

Husband's occupation in 1969	White		Nonwhite	
	Number of children ever born (per 1,000)	Percentage of husbands[a]	Number of children ever born (per 1,000)	Percentage of husbands[a]
All employed	3,101	93.4	3,813	88.5
Professional, technical, etc.	2,885	16.4	2,632	6.3
Managers, administrators, etc. (nonfarm)	2,981	14.3	3,039	3.2
Sales workers	2,934	6.8	2,992	1.4
Clerical, etc.	2,876	5.6	3,232	6.8
Craftsmen, etc.	3,181	22.8	3,816	16.0
Operatives (non-transport)	3,237	10.5	4,007	17.3
Transport operators	3,340	5.5	3,995	10.7
Laborers (nonfarm)	3,407	3.3	4,215	12.4
Farmers and farm managers	3,584	2.8	5,865	0.6
Farm laborers	4,197	0.8	6,354	2.5
Service workers (including private household)	3,070	4.6	3,554	11.3
Unemployed	3,447	1.8	4,355	2.7
In Armed Forces	3,080	2.1	3,349	2.1
Not in labor force	3,427	2.7	4,305	6.6
All occupations	3,116	100.0	3,851	99.9

a   Total percentage does not equal 100.0 because of rounding.
Source: U.S. Bureau of the Census (1973, Tables 46 and 47).

A cohort effect might also be the product of a depression. Children born during a depression might tend to be conservative about
their own fertility, preferring the certainty of being able to provide

Table 45. Number of children ever born to married women, by family income in 1969 and by presence of wife in labor force, for women 35–39 years old in 1970, and percentage of wives in each income category: United States

Family income (in 1970 U.S. dollars)	All married women		Wife in labor force	
	Number of children ever born (per 1,000)	Percentage of wives[a]	Number of children ever born (per 1,000)	Percentage of wives[a]
Less than $2,000	3,714	1.9	3,310	1.0
$2,000–$3,999	3,937	3.1	3,668	2.1
$4,000–$4,999	3,716	2.5	3,428	1.8
$5,000–$5,999	3,549	3.7	3,351	2.7
$6,000–$6,999	3,446	4.7	3,321	3.5
$7,000–$9,999	3,266	20.4	3,093	17.5
$10,000–$14,999	3,107	35.5	2,899	39.7
$15,000–$24,999	2,950	22.4	2,703	27.3
$25,000+	2,957	5.7	2,516	4.5
All incomes	3,181	99.9	2,919	100.1

a   Total percentage does not equal 100.0 because of rounding.

Source: U.S. Bureau of the Census (1973, Table 52).

for relatively few children to the risks of having many children when the economic weather might worsen once more. Thus, in spite of economic good times, they might have small completed families. Another cohort living through the same economic good times might take advantage of the prosperous conditions to have larger families. The resulting overall period fertility might be high, low, or average, but it would be composed of cohorts having different patterns and levels of fertility.

There is no guarantee that measures of period fertility and measures of cohort fertility referring to the same time span will show the same trends. An interesting example is presented by Barclay, using data for Taiwan in the 1933–52 period (Barclay, 1958: pp. 184–88). During that period, the total fertility rate changed as follows:

Calendar year period	Total fertility rate
1933–42	7,400
1938–47	6,850
1948–52	6,250

These period rates show declining fertility. Cohort measures for the same time, however, show a different pattern:

Birth cohort of women	Average number of children ever born
1888–92	6.90
1893–97	6.90
1898–1902	7.25
1903–07	7.35

The cohort measures indicate rising fertility. Both sets of measures are correct, but they refer to different groupings of women.

How discrepancies like the one for Taiwan occur can be clarified by a simple artificial example. Suppose we have the following age-specific rates:

Birth cohort	Age-specific fertility rates at ages:		
	15–24	25–34	35–44
1891–1900	50	300	200
1901–10	70	300	180
1911–20	110	300	180
1921–30	90	300	220

If we assume that all the births occurred to women 15–44 years old and that there was no mortality, we can make the following statements:

(1) In 1935, the women born in 1911–20 were 15–24; the women of the 1901–10 cohort were 25–34; and the women of the 1891–1900 cohort were 35–44. Hence, the three figures on the major diagonal represent the fertility for the year 1935. The total fertility rate for that year was 6,100.[10] Similarly, the total fertility rate for 1945 was 5,700. These two rates indicate a decrease in fertility.

(2) Although the period total fertility rates declined between 1935 and 1945, the cohort rates were successively higher:

1891–1900:	5,500
1901–10:	5,500
1911–20:	5,900
1921–30:	6,100

---

10 Since we are using ten-year age groups, the total fertility rate is the sum of the age-specific rates multiplied by ten.

This example demonstrates that it is possible to have period rates that change in one direction and, at the same time, cohort cumulative rates that change in the opposite direction. Such a paradox results from differences in the timing of births for the separate cohorts, which can produce unusually low or high points while the basic cohort trend is in a direction not indicated by the period rates.

In the example just given, the age pattern of childbearing changed during successive birth cohorts, and the change produced a discrepancy between cohort rates and period rates. Such discrepancies are quite possible if there have been shifts in the ages at which women marry, or if women plan and control their fertility and there have been outside causes (the economic depression mentioned earlier, for example) that lead to postponement of childbearing. That is, women born between 1891 and 1920 had an increasing proportion of their children in the earlier childbearing years. Women born after 1920 began having more children in their later childbearing years.

Eighth Set of Multiple-Choice Questions

1. Cohort fertility analyses:
   (a) have essentially the same use as the net reproduction rate.
   (b) have essentially the same use as the gross reproduction rate.
   (c) have the advantage of linking current and future fertility rates to past fertility histories of each cohort.
   (d) are useful only for populations in which contraception is not widely used.
   (e) refer to the experience of Roman military cohorts.

2. The chief difficulty with the net reproduction rate as a predictive device for population growth is that it:
   (a) excludes the influence of fertility.
   (b) makes inadequate allowance for mortality.
   (c) is based on the rates of a single year.
   (d) overlooks the type of culture possessed by the population.
   (e) only includes survivors of births in some past period.

3. Period birth rates and cohort birth rates may exhibit large differences under which of the following conditions?
   (a) When most couples plan their fertility.
   (b) When the mean age at marriage is increasing.
   (c) When the mean age at marriage is decreasing.
   (d) Two of the above.
   (e) All of the above.

4. Assuming there were no deaths to children or women in the past
   five years, one-fifth of the child-woman ratio should be approximately equal to:
   (a) the average general fertility rate for the past five years.
   (b) the total fertility rate for 7.5 years ago.
   (c) the crude birth rate for some indeterminate past period.
   (d) the average gross reproduction rate for the past five years.
   (e) the average net reproduction rate for the past five years.

Analysis of Birth Intervals

A final type of fertility analysis that is becoming increasingly important in the demographic literature is measuring the length of time
between successive births. As stated by Rindfuss et al. (1982: p. 5),
the increasing importance of such measures is due to the fact that:

> ... the fertility process is itself a sequential and time-dependent process.
> Birth interval analysis allows more precision in investigating many funda-
> mental questions; it allows the assessment of the effects of intermediate
> variables, like contraceptive use or lactation, and the explication of the
> effects of various socioeconomic variables in terms of intermediate
> variables.

Methods for properly analyzing birth intervals are still under development, because three complex methodological problems are associated
with birth interval analysis.

The first problem has to do with the quality of the data available
for studying birth intervals. Misdating of births or failure to remember their occurrence can reduce the data quality.

The second problem has to do with what has become known as
"censoring." Censoring occurs when birth intervals are interrupted
by data collection, such as in a sample survey. These intervals are
referred to as "open" intervals. Many of the open intervals will eventually be closed by a subsequent birth, but the timing of that closure
is unknown to the person analyzing the birth interval data. Analysis
of only the open intervals or only the closed intervals leads to analytic bias because open intervals tend to be longer than closed intervals, partly because some of the open intervals will never be closed
by another birth. The usual solution to this problem has been to use
life table techniques, with the next birth treated as a "death" and
the initial cohort consisting of women who have had the immediately
preceding birth. That is, women of parity n who have not yet given

birth to a child of order $n + 1$ are like persons of age x who have not yet died.

An illustration of this life table approach is provided in Table 46, adapted from an article by Bumpass et al. (1982) that analyzes data from the 1973 National Demographic Survey of the Philippines and the 1974 Korean World Fertility Survey. In the top panel of the table, the proportion of women who gave birth is presented tabulated by whether or not contraception had been used during the interval and by the duration of the interval. These figures are the equivalent of q_x values. For example, the figure .14 in the first cell of the table is the probability that a Korean woman who used contraception would have a second birth within the first 20 months after having her first birth.

Comparing women who used contraception with those who did not—i.e., by looking at the proportionate reduction in birth probabilities in the second panel of the table—we can make several observations:

(1) The effect of having used contraception is usually distinctly lower in the first duration segment (0–20 months) than in the second duration segment.

(2) Except for the first duration segment, the likely use of contraception for spacing purposes is indicated by the declining "effect" of having used contraception with increasing duration.

(3) Among Korean women at higher parities, there is an impressive reduction in fertility with contraceptive use.

The third problem in analyzing birth intervals has to do with the selectivity of the birth intervals available for analysis. Selectivity is particularly evident with sample survey data because surveys typically have restricted age ranges of those interviewed as well as restrictions by marital status or other criteria.

A hypothetical survey conducted in 1971 illustrates the problem. Table 47 shows the birth intervals that would be available for analysis in a survey of all ever married women under age 50. The horizontal dimension of the table indicates the age of the women at the time of the interview; the vertical dimension represents the age of the women at the start of a birth interval. Each cell of the table represents the year in which a birth interval began. The years are shown with the leading 19s omitted; i.e., "46" is 1946. Diagonals from top

Table 46. Birth probabilities within successive birth intervals 2, 3, and 4—8, by duration of interval and contraceptive use status: Philippines and Republic of Korea

Duration of interval and whether contraception used or not	Interval 2		Interval 3		Intervals 4—8	
	Korea	Philippines	Korea	Philippines	Korea	Philippines
Proportion giving birth during interval segment						
≤ 20 months						
Yes	.14	.28	.03	.23	.02	.19
No	.23	.43	.13	.32	.09	.26
21—26 months						
Yes	.21	.20	.08	.14	.04	.11
No	.41	.40	.31	.36	.19	.29
27—32 months						
Yes	.28	.21	.15	.17	.07	.11
No	.42	.35	.44	.35	.31	.28
33—44 months						
Yes	.45	.48	.36	.36	.12	.20
No	.59	.50	.67	.48	.46	.42
Proportionate reduction in birth probability due to contraceptive use[a] $\left(\dfrac{P_{no} - P_{yes}}{P_{no}}\right)$						
≤ 20 months	.39	.35	.74	.29	.84	.29
21—26 months	.48	.50	.73	.60	.79	.62
27—32 months	.34	.38	.66	.53	.77	.61
33—44 months	.22	.03	.47	.26	.75	.52
Number of cases						
≤ 20 months						
Yes	348	141	577	216	1,928	740
No	1,724	1,779	1,308	1,608	2,917	5,491
21—26 months						
Yes	288	96	526	156	1,862	569
No	1,304	1,005	1,114	1,081	2,622	4,001
27—32 months						
Yes	202	62	439	118	1,685	441
No	743	570	751	677	2,073	2,716
33—44 months						
Yes	132	40	312	77	1,395	325
No	404	351	399	411	1,361	1,840

Note: The first interval is between marriage and the first birth, the second interval is between the first and second births, etc.

a   Proportions in second panel calculated from unrounded figures.

Source: Bumpass et al. (1982:248).

left to bottom right of the table represent the birth intervals begun in a given year.

The solid triangle encloses the intervals actually available for analysis. Notice, first, that intervals begun at age 15 could have been initiated in any year between 1937 and 1971, whereas intervals begun at age 49 could start only in 1971. The time periods represented are different for different ages at initiation. Second, notice that comparison of birth cohorts (each column in the table) shows that the cohorts vary considerably in the possible ages at beginning of the interval. At the extremes, women of age 49 could have initiated an interval at any age from 15 to 49. Women of age 15 could have initiated an interval only at 15. Third, look at the different time periods during which the birth intervals were begun. Intervals begun before 1947, for example, had to be initiated at age 25 or younger. Intervals begun before 1940 had to be initiated at age 18 or younger.

The three points above clearly illustrate biases introduced by selectivity. If age at the beginning of an interval, birth cohort, and time period were all unrelated to fertility, these biases could be ignored. Unfortunately, all three of these variables are known to be highly related to fertility.

The principal question introduced by selectivity biases is: Of those birth intervals available for analysis, which should be analyzed? There is no single solution, and a full treatment of the selectivity issue is beyond the scope of this *Guide*. Readers interested in pursuing the matter further should read Rodriguez and Hobcraft (1980) and Rindfuss et al. (1982).

Ninth Set of Multiple Choice Questions

1. Censoring refers to the fact that:
   (a) women often forget the exact dates of birth of their children.
   (b) at the time of data collection, some women have not completed childbearing.
   (c) not all women in the population are interviewed.
   (d) data for some countries are suppressed by the government.
   (e) b and c above are correct.
2. Selectivity biases in survey data:
   (a) are only important in the analysis of birth intervals.
   (b) may affect studies of the intervals between marriages, geographic movements, or job changes.

Table 47. Year in which any birth interval had to begin, given age at 1971: all intervals

Age at beginning of interval	Age at time of interview																									
	15	16	17	18	19	20	21	22	23	24	25	26	27	28	29	30	31	32	33	34	35	36	37	38	39	40
15	71	70	69	68	67	66	65	64	63	62	61	60	59	58	57	56	55	54	53	52	51	50	49	48	47	46
16		71	70	69	68	67	66	65	64	63	62	61	60	59	58	57	56	55	54	53	52	51	50	49	48	47
17			71	70	69	68	67	66	65	64	63	62	61	60	59	58	57	56	55	54	53	52	51	50	49	48
18				71	70	69	68	67	66	65	64	63	62	61	60	59	58	57	56	55	54	53	52	51	50	49
19					71	70	69	68	67	66	65	64	63	62	61	60	59	58	57	56	55	54	53	52	51	50
20						71	70	69	68	67	66	65	64	63	62	61	60	59	58	57	56	55	54	53	52	51
21							71	70	69	68	67	66	65	64	63	62	61	60	59	58	57	56	55	54	53	52
22								71	70	69	68	67	66	65	64	63	62	61	60	59	58	57	56	55	54	53
23									71	70	69	68	67	66	65	64	63	62	61	60	59	58	57	56	55	54
24										71	70	69	68	67	66	65	64	63	62	61	60	59	58	57	56	55
25											71	70	69	68	67	66	65	64	63	62	61	60	59	58	57	56
26												71	70	69	68	67	66	65	64	63	62	61	60	59	58	57
27													71	70	69	68	67	66	65	64	63	62	61	60	59	58
28														71	70	69	68	67	66	65	64	63	62	61	60	59
29															71	70	69	68	67	66	65	64	63	62	61	60
30																71	70	69	68	67	66	65	64	63	62	61
31																	71	70	69	68	67	66	65	64	63	62
32																		71	70	69	68	67	66	65	64	63
33																			71	70	69	68	67	66	65	64
34																				71	70	69	68	67	66	65
35																					71	70	69	68	67	66
36																						71	70	69	68	67
37																							71	70	69	68
38																								71	70	69
39																									71	70
40																										71
41																										
42																										
43																										
44																										
45																										
46																										
47																										
48																										
49																										

beginning of interval and age at interview, for a survey taking place in

```
41 42 43 44 45 46 47 48 49 50 51 52 53 54 55 56 57 58 59 60 61 62 63 64 65 66 67 68 69

45 44 43 42 41 40 39 38 37|36 35 34 33 32 31 30 29 28 27 26 25 24 23 22 21 20 19 18 17
46 45 44 43 42 41 40 39 38|37 36 35 34 33 32 31 30 29 28 27 26 25 24 23 22 21 20 19 18
47 46 45 44 43 42 41 40 39|38 37 36 35 34 33 32 31 30 29 28 27 26 25 24 23 22 21 20 19
48 47 46 45 44 43 42 41 40|39 38 37 36 35 34 33 32 31 30 29 28 27 26 25 24 23 22 21 20
49 48 47 46 45 44 43 42 41|40 39 38 37 36 35 34 33 32 31 30 29 28 27 26 25 24 23 22 21
50 49 48 47 46 45 44 43 42|41 40 39 38 37 36 35 34 33 32 31 30 29 28 27 26 25 24 23 22
51 50 49 48 47 46 45 44 43|42 41 40 39 38 37 36 35 34 33 32 31 30 29 28 27 26 25 24 23
52 51 50 49 48 47 46 45 44|43 42 41 40 39 38 37 36 35 34 33 32 31 30 29 28 27 26 25 24
53 52 51 50 49 48 47 46 45|44 43 42 41 40 39 38 37 36 35 34 33 32 31 30 29 28 27 26 25
54 53 52 51 50 49 48 47 46|45 44 43 42 41 40 39 38 37 36 35 34 33 32 31 30 29 28 27 26
55 54 53 52 51 50 49 48 47|46 45 44 43 42 41 40 39 38 37 36 35 34 33 32 31 30 29 28 27
56 55 54 53 52 51 50 49 48|47 46 45 44 43 42 41 40 39 38 37 36 35 34 33 32 31 30 29 28
57 56 55 54 53 52 51 50 49|48 47 46 45 44 43 42 41 40 39 38 37 36 35 34 33 32 31 30 29
58 57 56 55 54 53 52 51 50|49 48 47 46 45 44 43 42 41 40 39 38 37 36 35 34 33 32 31 30
59 58 57 56 55 54 53 52 51|50 49 48 47 46 45 44 43 42 41 40 39 38 37 36 35 34 33 32 31
60 59 58 57 56 55 54 53 52|51 50 49 48 47 46 45 44 43 42 41 40 39 38 37 36 35 34 33 32
61 60 59 58 57 56 55 54 53|52 51 50 49 48 47 46 45 44 43 42 41 40 39 38 37 36 35 34 33
62 61 60 59 58 57 56 55 54|53 52 51 50 49 48 47 46 45 44 43 42 41 40 39 38 37 36 35 34
63 62 61 60 59 58 57 56 55|54 53 52 51 50 49 48 47 46 45 44 43 42 41 40 39 38 37 36 35
64 63 62 61 60 59 58 57 56|55 54 53 52 51 50 49 48 47 46 45 44 43 42 41 40 39 38 37 36
65 64 63 62 61 60 59 58 57|56 55 54 53 52 51 50 49 48 47 46 45 44 43 42 41 40 39 38 37
66 65 64 63 62 61 60 59 58|57 56 55 54 53 52 51 50 49 48 47 46 45 44 43 42 41 40 39 38
67 66 65 64 63 62 61 60 59|58 57 56 55 54 53 52 51 50 49 48 47 46 45 44 43 42 41 40 39
68 67 66 65 64 63 62 61 60|59 58 57 56 55 54 53 52 51 50 49 48 47 46 45 44 43 42 41 40
69 68 67 66 65 64 63 62 61|60 59 58 57 56 55 54 53 52 51 50 49 48 47 46 45 44 43 42 41
70 69 68 67 66 65 64 63 62|61 60 59 58 57 56 55 54 53 52 51 50 49 48 47 46 45 44 43 42
71 70 69 68 67 66 65 64 63|62 61 60 59 58 57 56 55 54 53 52 51 50 49 48 47 46 45 44 43
   71 70 69 68 67 66 65 64|63 62 61 60 59 58 57 56 55 54 53 52 51 50 49 48 47 46 45 44
      71 70 69 68 67 66 65|64 63 62 61 60 59 58 57 56 55 54 53 52 51 50 49 48 47 46 45
         71 70 69 68 67 66|65 64 63 62 61 60 59 58 57 56 55 54 53 52 51 50 49 48 47 46
            71 70 69 68 67|66 65 64 63 62 61 60 59 58 57 56 55 54 53 52 51 50 49 48 47
               71 70 69 68|67 66 65 64 63 62 61 60 59 58 57 56 55 54 53 52 51 50 49 48
                  71 70 69|68 67 66 65 64 63 62 61 60 59 58 57 56 55 54 53 52 51 50 49
                     71 70|69 68 67 66 65 64 63 62 61 60 59 58 57 56 55 54 53 52 51 50
                        71|70 69 68 67 66 65 64 63 62 61 60 59 58 57 56 55 54 53 52 51
```

(c)   arise because women often forget the exact ages of birth of their children.

(d)   arise because the survey is cross-sectional rather than a complete longitudinal study of each birth cohort of women.

(e)   b and d above are correct.

(f)   a and c above are correct.

3. Open birth intervals are likely:
   (a)   to be longer than closed birth intervals.
   (b)   to be shorter than closed birth intervals.
   (c)   to be about the same length as closed birth intervals.

4. Selectivity biases refer to biases introduced by selectivity on:
   (a)   age at the initiation of a birth interval.
   (b)   time period.
   (c)   birth cohort.
   (d)   all of the above.
   (e)   none of the above.

Additional Reading

The literature on fertility analysis is growing rapidly. Consequently, the works mentioned here are necessarily selective and do not adequately reflect the diversity of the literature. Further discussion of the methods described in this chapter can be found in several of the sources listed in Chapter 2. You may also wish to consult:

United Nations Statistical Office, Department of Economic and Social Affairs, Population Bulletin No. 7, *With Special Reference to the Situation and Recent Trends of Fertility in the World.* (New York: United Nations, 1965).

Donald J. Bogue, *Principles of Demography* (New York: John Wiley and Sons, Inc., 1969), especially chapters 5 and 18.

Most books of readings on population have one or more chapters on fertility as do most textbooks on demography. New methods for constructing fertility rates from deficient data are being developed regularly. Bogue and Palmore (1964), Palmore (1978), and Cho (1964), mentioned earlier in this chapter, are illustrative. Prominent methods include the "own-children method" developed principally by Lee-Jay Cho and colleagues, the "Brass methods" developed by William Brass and others, and the regression techniques developed by James Palmore and others that were referred to earlier in this chapter.

Additional materials on the use of both fertility and mortality measures can be found through judicious sampling of appropriate journals, including:

Asian and Pacific Census Forum
Demography
Family Planning Perspectives
Genus
International Family Planning Perspectives
Population
Population and Development Review
Population and Environment
Population Index
Population Studies
Social Biology
Studies in Family Planning
Theoretical Population Biology

Many journals that do not focus specifically on population studies also carry articles of interest.

Appendix 1
Notation and Formulas

Many systems of notation are found in the various demographic texts and writings. Although the meaning of symbols will usually be clear from the context, variability in notation can result in some confusion. In this volume we have endeavored to use a consistent system of notation, based upon that of the life table. Readers should be aware that in some cases our system is different than that found in the literature. We believe that the consistency we have introduced makes up for this.

In demography, we use letters to stand for a number of events or persons. Thus, a "B" is used to represent the number of births, a "D" to represent the number of deaths, and a "P" to represent the number of people in the population. (Note that the letter often represents the first letter of the word for the concept we are symbolizing, but this is not always the case.) Small letters are also used: "d" stands for the number of deaths in a life table population.

Subscripts and superscripts are common in demographic notation. Perhaps the most common is the subscript "x", which usually stands for exact age at the beginning of an age interval. "D_x" refers to all deaths to persons x to $x + 1$ years of age, whereas D_{18} refers to deaths to all persons who became 18 on their last birthday (which is the same as saying all persons of exact age 18 to exact age 19). Another common subscript is "n", which often refers to the size of an age interval: "$_nP_x^f$" refers to all women of ages x to $x + n$. Thus, $_5P_{20}^f$ refers to all women of ages 20 through 24—i.e., an age interval of five years. If $n = 1$, it is often not written: $D_{18} = {}_1D_{18}$.

In this volume we use superscripts mainly to designate sex: P^f

refers to the female population, P^m to the male population. Superscripts may also be used to refer to a date or period of time: P^{1975} would be the 1975 population count or estimate.

Two other symbols need mention here. One is *"k"*, which is short for "konstant" and refers to a constant by which many "raw" demographic measures are multiplied to make them easier to understand. For example, the crude birth rate in a country may be 0.012 per year. This is good demographic description but not as easy for many people to understand as if it were multiplied by a constant, $k = 1,000$. The crude birth rate is then 12, or 12 *per 1,000,* and that is how it is usually expressed. Similarly, the growth rate is often expressed as a percentage—i.e., in this case, $k = 100$.

The other symbol is the summation sign, Σ, which is the Greek letter S (for sum). It is used in demography to indicate that the expression following it is to be summed. Thus, for example, the notation

$$\sum_{x=0}^{x=49} P_x$$

means: Take the sum of the population at each age from 0 through 49, i.e., $P_0 + P_1 + P_2 + \ldots + P_{48} + P_{49}$.

Keeping these conventions and rules in mind, we present a list of concepts defined in this volume and the formulas used to describe them algebraically.

Concept	Formula	Discussed on pages
MORTALITY		
Crude death rate (CDR)	$M = \dfrac{D}{P} k$	9–10
Age-specific death rate (ASDR) (for exact ages x to $x + n$)	$_nM_x = \dfrac{_nD_x}{_nP_x} k$	10, 12
Age-standardized death rate (for population B with A as standard)	$M^* = \dfrac{\sum\limits_{x} (_nP_x^A)(_nM_x^B)}{\sum\limits_{x} {_nP_x^A}} k$	18–26
Infant mortality rate (IMR)	$IMR = \dfrac{D_0}{B} k$	28–31

Concept	Formula	Discussed on pages
LIFE TABLE		
Probability of dying between exact ages x and $x+n$	$_nq_x$	35–41
Number of deaths between exact ages x and $x+n$	$_nd_x$	41
Survivors to exact age x	ℓ_x	41–42
Years lived between exact ages x and $x+n$	$_nL_x$	42–44
Total years lived after exact age x	T_x	44
Expectation of life after exact age x	e_x	44–45

Relationships among columns of the life table

$$_nq_x = \frac{_nd_x}{\ell_x}$$

$$_nd_x = \ell_x - \ell_{x+n}$$

$$_nL_x = \frac{n}{2}(\ell_x + \ell_{x+n}) \quad \text{(except at youngest and oldest ages)}$$

$$T_x = \sum_{x=i}^{w} L_i, \text{ where } w \text{ refers to the last ("open") age interval}$$

$$e_x = \frac{T_x}{\ell_x}$$

Life table birth rate (b) = life table death rate (d) = $\dfrac{\ell_0}{T_0}$ 47

FERTILITY, NATURAL INCREASE, AND REPRODUCTION RATES

Crude birth rate (CBR)	$\text{CBR} = \dfrac{B}{P}k$	61
Crude rate of natural increase (CRNI)	$\text{CRNI} = \dfrac{B-D}{P}k$	64

Concept	Formula	Discussed on pages
General fertility rate (GFR)	$\text{GFR} = \dfrac{B}{{}_{30}P^f_{15}}\, k \ \text{ or } \ \dfrac{B}{{}_{35}P^f_{15}}\, k$	68–69
Age-specific fertility rate (ASFR) (for exact ages x to $x+n$)	${}_nF_x = \dfrac{{}_nB_x}{{}_nP^f_x}\, k$	69–71
Birth order-specific fertility rate	${}_nF^i_x = \dfrac{{}_nB^i_x}{{}_nP^f_x}\, k$	76–77
Total fertility rate (TFR)	$\text{TFR} = n\sum\limits_x {}_nF_x$	84–88
Gross reproduction rate (GRR)	$\text{GRR} = n\sum\limits_x {}_nF^f_x$	88–90
Net reproduction rate (NRR)	$\text{NRR} = \sum\limits_x ({}_nF^f_x)\left(\dfrac{{}_nL^f_x}{\ell_0}\right)$	90–94
Child-woman ratio (CWR)	$\text{CWR} = \dfrac{{}_5P_0}{{}_{30}P^f_{15}}\, k \ \text{ or } \ \dfrac{{}_5P_0}{{}_{35}P^f_{15}}\, k$	103–104

where: B = births
D = deaths
P = population
P^f = female population
x = exact age
n = size of age interval
i = order of birth, and
k = a constant

Appendix 2
Relationship between q_x and M_x Values

Constructing a life table for a real population depends upon determining the values of the q_x function from observed values of age-specific death rates (which are symbolized by M_x in our notation). The q_x values differ from the age-specific death rates (M_x) that we have discussed earlier in the following ways:

(1) In the q_x values, the denominator includes members of only one (hypothetical) birth cohort, whereas in the age-specific death rate (M_x), the denominator includes members of more than one (real) birth cohort. For example, the persons in the age group of exact age 4 to exact age 5 in midyear 1969 would include some persons born in 1964 and some born in 1965. The denominator for the age-specific death rate, hence, includes parts of both the 1964 and 1965 birth cohorts.

(2) In the q_x values, the numerator includes members of only one birth cohort, whereas in the age-specific death rate (M_x) the numerator includes members of more than one birth cohort. For example, the persons who died at age 4 in 1969 would include some persons born in 1964 and some persons born in 1965.

(3) For the denominator of the age-specific death rate (M_x), we use the midyear population as an estimate of the number of person-years lived. The midyear population is a biased estimate of the number of persons exposed to the risk of dying to the extent that it excludes persons who died during the first half of the year. Further, for life table purposes it is biased because it

includes persons who migrated into the population during the year—and migration is expressly omitted in the life table calculations.

Usually, age-specific death rates (M_x) overestimate the probabilities of dying during a given exact age interval (q_x) because they exclude persons dying in the first half of the year from the denominator and because they refer on the average to persons $x + \frac{1}{2}$ years old instead of x years old.

Rather complex methods have been developed for calculating q_x values from M_x values, most of which are well beyond the scope of this *Guide.* An approximate value for q_x can be found for ages over 4, however, on the assumption that:

$$q_x = \frac{M_x}{1 + \frac{1}{2}M_x}.$$

This is the most common formula for calculating values for q_x (except for the first few years of life), although various methods of adjusting the values of M_x are often used before the basic formula is applied.

For the younger ages, particularly exact age 0, the determination of q_x is especially problematic. Often, the infant mortality rate is used directly as the value of q_0 in a life table. The defect in the infant mortality rate is the same in principle as that for death rates at other ages—i.e., more than one cohort is involved in the numerator—but it is more serious because births (the denominator of the IMR) may fluctuate rather dramatically from year to year. It is sometimes possible to obtain a satisfactory degree of precision by averaging over several years. For example, we might calculate the infant mortality rate by dividing the number of deaths to infants in years 1975, 1976, and 1977 by the number of births occurring in those same years. This provides more accuracy than the usual method of calculating the infant mortality rate because the deaths in the numerator are matched with the proper set of births in the denominator except at the beginning and the end of the period.

Another method of calculating q_0 involves determining the number of children who were born in each month and also the deaths of children by age in months at death. With these data, it is possible to construct a rate such that the numerator and denominator both refer to the same cohort. There are also methods for estimating this type of rate, but we omit a technical discussion here. The interested reader can refer to the more advanced sources cited in the concluding section of Chapter 2. The more precise techniques for estimating infant mortality rates discussed in those sources are already of the type used in the life table, and consequently no further adjustment is required. For ages 1 to 4, similar techniques are often employed, although the use of the simple formula given above for ages over 4 is often used to convert values of M_1 through M_4 into the appropriate q_x values.

Appendix 3
Answers to Selected Exercises

Exercise 2 *(page 10)*
1. Where did the deaths occur? How many people were exposed to the risk of dying?
2. Only the population size for the end of the year is given. This is usually an inadequate measure of the number of persons exposed to the risk of dying during the year.
3. When did they die?

First Set of Multiple-Choice Questions *(pages 17–18)*
1. (d)—cannot tell without knowledge of the age structure.
2. (c)—cannot tell for certain without knowledge of the age structure.

Second Set of Multiple-Choice Questions *(page 27)*
1. (a)—the age-specific rates for country *A* are higher in every age group.
2. (b)—see Table 3.
3. (a).
4. (b)—see Table 1.

Exercise 3 *(page 28)*
Case 1: The differentials in the crude death rates are not a result of age distribution differentials. City *B* had about the same average mortality levels as the United States as a whole, but City *A* had substantially higher mortality levels than either City *B* or the United States.

Case 2: City *A* and City *B* both had substantially higher mortality levels than the United States when age differentials are taken into account, and the two cities were very similar in their mortality levels. City *B* probably had a younger age distribution than either the United States or City *A* and that accounts for its lower crude death rate.

Case 3: The mortality rates of the two cities were on the average closely similar to that of the United States as a whole. Since City *B* apparently had an age structure similar to that of the United States, this mortality similarity to the United States is reflected in either the crude or standardized rate comparisons. City A must have had an older population than either City B or the United States, however, because its higher mortality as reflected in comparisons of the crude death rate disappears in comparisons with age standardized.

Case 4: When age is taken into account by standardization, it appears that City A had mortality levels like those of the United States but City B had substantially higher mortality rates than either City A or the United States. This reverses the comparative mortality levels of the crude death rates. Therefore, it is likely that City A had an old population, which gave it a high crude death rate, despite low age-specific mortality rates. By the same logic City B must have had a very young population, which gave it a relatively low crude death rate even though on the average its age-specific death rates were relatively high.

Case 5: Once age is controlled by standardization, it appears that City B had slightly higher mortality levels and City A still higher mortality levels than the United States. City B must have had a somewhat younger population than the United States or at least one that had somewhat less concentration in higher mortality age groups, because initially the crude death rate was equal to that of the United States, and standardization makes it a little higher. City A must have had a significantly older population than either City B or the United States, because the overall mortality differential as compared with the United States or City B is reduced (but not eliminated) when an age adjustment is made.

Case 6: Age differentials obscure the probable average mortality differentials among the three populations. The fact that City A had lower mortality levels than either City B or the United States (in age-standardized comparisons) must be obscured in the crude rate comparisons by the fact that City A's age structure must have been very different from that of the other populations. Presumably, it had an old age structure, because standardization reduces its rate by more than 50 percent whereas it only slightly increases the rate for City B.

Exercise 4 *(page 28)*

Rate	Country A	Country B
Crude death rate	38.25	32.25
Death rate standardized on distribution for		
Country A	38.25	43.25
Country B	27.25	32.25

Country B's lower crude death rate results from the fact that a large part of its population lives in the metropolitan areas, where death rates are relatively low. Country A initially has a high crude death rate, despite its low mortality within each type of region, because there is a population concentration in the high mortality rural areas.

First Set of True-False Questions *(pages 31–32)*
1. True.
2. False, because of the younger age structure in the developing countries.
3. False.
4. False. It is not if events have occurred unevenly throughout the year.
5. False also for infants; i.e., death rates are highest at the extreme ages for both young and old.

Third Set of Multiple-Choice Questions *(pages 50–51)*
1. (a).
2. (c)–because death rate = ℓ_0/T_0 and $e_0 = T_0/\ell_0 = 1/$death rate.
3. (b).
4. (d)–because a probability has all persons at the start of a period in the denominator, whereas a death rate has the total number of person years lived–which, in the absence of migration, must be less than those at the start, unless there is no mortality at all.
5. (b).
6. (d).

Second Set of True-False Questions *(pages 51–52)*
1. True.
2. False. They are equal.
3. True.
4. True.

Fourth Set of Multiple-Choice Questions *(page 56)*
1. (f)
2. (e)–and not (d), because (c) is true for the reason that q_x determines ℓ_x.

Third Set of True-False Questions *(page 57)*
1. False. Death rates at these ages are relatively high.
2. True.
3. False.
4. False. Life tables refer to groups, not individuals, and they refer to *real* groups (not hypothetical groups) only if mortality rates are not changing or the life table in question is a generational life table.
5. Arguable. Crude death rates do measure the actual rate of mortality of the population as it is at a moment of time. They do not measure mortality independently of the effect of the age distribution. Therefore, the standardized rates are better if you want to compare the underlying population trends. The crude rates are preferable if you want to

measure the rate at which the population is dying without reference to whether age has affected it.
6. True.

Fourth Set of True-False Questions *(pages 72, 74)*
1. Probably false, but data for mainland China are not known.
2. True—if United Nations and other estimates are correct.
3. True.
4. False.
5. True.

Fifth Set of Multiple-Choice Questions *(pages 74—75)*
1. (e).
2. (b).
3. (b).
4. (d).
5. (b).
6. (b).

Sixth Set of Multiple-Choice Questions *(pages 82—84)*
1. (d).
2. (d).
3. (c).
4. (b).

Fifth Set of True-False Questions *(page 84)*
1. True.
2. True.
3. False.
4. True.

Exercise 5 *(page 99)*
The exact results will depend on the particular changes made. However, any shift that raises birth rates at younger ages and also makes an equal reduction in birth rates at older ages should have the effect of:

(a) decreasing the length of a generation, because the average age of mothers at the birth of their children will be less.

(b) increasing the net reproduction rate insofar as mortality will be less at younger ages. In a population such as that of the United States, this shift will not be of great importance since mortality is low at all ages of the reproductive span, and the net and gross reproduction rates are nearly the same.

Exercise 6 *(page 100)*
Country *A:* Both fertility and mortality are low because both the net and

gross reproduction rates are low, and the difference between them is small. If the current age-specific birth and death rates continue indefinitely, the population size will decline slowly, eventually stabilizing at the rate of 15 per thousand per generation. Since the birth and death rates are equal and the birth rate is low, it appears likely (but not certain) that the age structure is not far from that required for this permanent condition.

Country *B:* The statements made about country *A* with respect to the net and gross reproduction rate apply here too. However, the fact that the crude birth rate is much higher than the crude death rate, with a substantial rate of present natural increase, makes it probable that the age structure is young (probably as a result of higher past fertility). Therefore, the attainment of the slow growth decline will take a long time, even if the age-specific vital rates continue at their present level. This situation is similar to the actual situation in Japan in recent years.

Country *C:* The high gross reproduction rate indicates very high fertility rates. That there is little difference between the net and gross rates means that mortality is very low. This is a population that will grow rapidly (195 percent per generation) if its current vital rates continue indefinitely. Unless it has an unusually old age structure, the crude birth rate is likely to be very high and the crude death rate very low at present. This would be characteristic of a population like the American Hutterites.

Country *D:* This is a country in which fertility and mortality are both very high. The large gross reproduction rate indicates that fertility is high. The fact that the net reproduction rate is so much lower means that mortality must be high. The net reproduction rate of 1,000 means that for the long run, mortality is sufficiently high to offset completely the high fertility. Long-run implications are a stationary population. That birth and death rates are currently equal at a high level suggests that this condition is already closely approximated.

Country *E:* Fertility rates are moderately high and mortality rates low. This inference follows from the fact that the gross reproduction rate is substantially above 1,000 (although there are many higher rates) and the net reproduction rate differs from it rather little. In the long run if the age-specific vital rates remain at their current levels, this population will grow at the rate of about 48 percent per generation. This is a situation rather similar to that in the United States during the period following World War II.

Country *F:* The country has high fertility and moderate mortality, because its very high gross reproduction rate and net reproduction rate differ from the gross rate moderately. (If mortality were very low, the net reproduction rate would differ very little from the gross rate. If mortality were very high, the net reproduction rate would be 1,000 or less.) Should these vital rates continue indefinitely, the growth rate per generation would be about 50 percent. The actual crude birth rate and death rates given are consistent

with a situation in which fertility remains high but mortality has fallen
from previously higher levels. This situation is probably representative of
a country like India or Pakistan.

Sixth Set of True-False Questions *(page 100)*
1. True.
2. False.
3. True.
4. True.
5. False.
6. False.
7. True.

Seventh Set of Multiple-Choice Questions *(pages 100–02)*
1. (c).
2. (c).
3. (c).
4. (d).
5. (c).
6. (d).

Eighth Set of Multiple-Choice Questions *(pages 111–12)*
1. (c).
2. (c).
3. (e).
4. (a).

Ninth Set of Multiple-Choice Questions *(pages 115, 118)*
1. (b).
2. (e).
3. (a).
4. (d).

References

Akers, Donald S.

    1967   On measuring the marriage squeeze. *Demography* 4(2):907–24.

Barclay, George W.

    1958   *Techniques of Population Analysis.* New York: John Wiley and Sons.

Bogue, Donald J.

    1969   *Principles of Demography.* New York: John Wiley and Sons.

Bogue, Donald J., and Evelyn Kitagawa

    n.d.   *Manual of Demographic Research Techniques* (in preparation). Community and Family Study Center, University of Chicago.

Bogue, Donald J., and James A. Palmore

    1964   Some empirical and analytic relations among demographic fertility measures, with regression models for fertility estimation. *Demography* 1(1):316–38.

Bumpass, Larry L., Ronald R. Rindfuss, James A. Palmore, Mercedes Concepción, and Byoung Mohk Choi

    1982   Intermediate variables and educational differentials in fertility in Korea and the Philippines. *Demography* 19(2):241–60.

Carr-Saunders, A.M.

    1936   *World Population.* Fair Lawn, N.J.: Oxford University Press.

Cho, Lee-Jay

    1964   Estimated refined measures of fertility for all major countries of the world. *Demography* 1(1):359–74.

Cho, Lee-Jay, and Man Jun Hahm

1968   Recent changes in fertility rates of the Korean population. *Demography* 5(2):690–98.

Cho, Lee-Jay, James A. Palmore, and Lyle Saunders

1968   Recent fertility trends in West Malaysia. *Demography* 5(2): 732–44.

Dublin, L.I., A.J. Lotka, and M. Spiegelman

1949   *Length of Life,* revised edition. New York: Ronald Press.

Durand, John D.

1968   The modern expansion of world population. In Charles B. Nam, ed., *Population and Society.* Boston: Houghton-Mifflin.

Easterlin, Richard, ed.

1980   *Population and Economic Change in Developing Countries.* Chicago: University of Chicago Press.

Eaton, Joseph W., and Albert J. Mayer

1954   *Man's Capacity to Reproduce: The Demography of a Unique Population.* Glencoe, Ill.: The Free Press.

Freedman, Ronald, and Arjun L. Adlakha

1968   Recent fertility declines in Hong Kong: the role of the changing age structure. *Population Studies* 22(2):181–98.

Greville, Thomas N.E.

1946   *United States Life Tables and Actuarial Tables, 1939–1941.* Washington, D.C.: U.S. Bureau of the Census.

Grove, Robert D., and Alice M. Hetzel

1968   *Vital Statistics Rates in the United States 1940–1960.* Washington, D.C.: U.S. Government Printing Office.

Hauser, Philip M.

1960   *Population Perspectives.* New Brunswick, N.J.: Rutgers University Press.

Jaffe, A.J.

1951   *Handbook of Statistical Methods for Demographers.* Washington, D.C.: U.S. Bureau of the Census.

Keyfitz, Nathan

1968   *Introduction to the Mathematics of Population.* Reading, Mass.: Addison-Wesley.

Keyfitz, Nathan, and Wilhelm Flieger

1968   *World Population: An Analysis of Vital Data.* Chicago: University of Chicago Press.

1971   *Population: Facts and Methods of Demography.* San Francisco: W.H. Freeman and Co.

Marty, Robert, and David J. Neebe

1966   *Compound Interest Tables: For Long-term Planning in Forestry.* U.S. Department of Agriculture Forest Service, Agriculture Handbook No. 311. Washington, D.C.: U.S. Government Printing Office.

Office of Population Research, Princeton University

1950   *Population Index* 16(2), April.

1961   *Population Index* 27(2), April.

1968   *Population Index* 34(2), April-June.

1979   *Population Index* 45(2), April.

1980a   *Population Index* 46(2), Summer.

1980b   *Population Index* 46(3), Fall.

1981   *Population Index* 47(2), Summer.

Palmore, James A.

1978   *Regression Estimates of Changes in Fertility, 1955–1960 to 1965–1975, for Most Major Nations and Territories.* No. 58, Papers of the East-West Population Institute. Honolulu: East-West Center.

Pressat, Roland

1972   *Demographic Analysis: Methods, Results, Applications.* New York: Aldine-Atherton.

Preston, Samuel H.

1976   *Mortality Patterns in National Patterns.* New York: Academic Press.

Preston, Samuel H., ed.

1978   *The Effects of Infant and Child Mortality on Fecundity.* New York: Academic Press.

Preston, Samuel H., Nathan Keyfitz, and Robert Schoen

1972   *Causes of Death: Life Tables for National Populations.* New York: Seminar Press.

138

Retherford, Robert D., and Lee-Jay Cho

1973   Comparative analysis of recent fertility trends in East Asia. Pp.
        163–81 in *Proceedings of the International Population Confer-
        ence, Liège, 1973.* Liège: International Union for the Scientific
        Study of Population.

Rindfuss, Ronald R., James A. Palmore, and Larry L. Bumpass

1982   Selectivity and the analysis of birth intervals using survey data.
        Asian and Pacific Census Forum 8(3):5–6, 8–10, 15–16.

Rodriguez, German, and John N. Hobcraft

1980   *Illustrative Analysis: Life Table Analysis of Birth Intervals in
        Colombia.* World Fertility Survey Scientific Reports, No. 16.
        London: World Fertility Survey.

Shryock, Henry, Jacob S. Siegel, and Associates

1971   *The Methods and Materials of Demography,* 2 vols. Washington,
        D.C.: U.S. Bureau of the Census. (Condensed version available
        from Academic Press, New York, 1978.)

Spiegelman, Mortimer

1968   *Introduction to Demography,* revised edition. Cambridge, Mass.:
        Harvard University Press.

Stycos, J. Mayone, and Kurt W. Back

1964   *The Control of Human Fertility in Jamaica.* Ithaca, N.Y.:
        Cornell University Press.

Thompson, Warren S., and David T. Lewis

1965   *Population Problems,* fifth edition. New York: McGraw-Hill.

United Nations Population Division, Department of Social Affairs

1973   *The Determinants and Consequences of Population Trends.*
        Population Studies, No. 50. New York: United Nations.

United Nations Statistical Office, Department of Economic and Social Affairs

1948–   *Demographic Yearbook.* Annual. New York: United Nations.

1955   *Principles for a Vital Statistics System.* Statistical Papers, Series
        M, No. 19. New York: United Nations.

1958   *Multilingual Demographic Dictionary.* Population Studies, No.
        29. New York: United Nations.

1962   *The Situation and Recent Trends of Mortality in the World.*
        Population Bulletin No. 6. New York: United Nations.

1965   *With Special Reference to the Situation and Recent Trends of
        Fertility in the World.* Population Bulletin No. 7. New York:
        United Nations.

1980   *World Population Trends and Policies,* 1979 Monitoring Report, Vol. 1. New York: United Nations.

U.S. Bureau of the Census, Department of Commerce

1960   *Historical Statistics of the United States: Colonial Times to 1957.* Washington, D.C.: U.S. Government Printing Office.

1966   Fertility of the population: June 1964 and March 1962. *Current Population Reports,* Series P-20, No. 147. Washington, D.C.: U.S. Government Printing Office.

1973   Women by number of children ever born. *Census of Population,* 1970 Special Report, Final Report PC(2)-3A. Washington, D.C.: U.S. Government Printing Office.

1977   *Country Demographic Profiles, Sri Lanka.* Washington, D.C.: U.S. Government Printing Office.

1979   Fertility of American women: June, 1978. *Current Population Reports,* Series P-20, No. 341. Washington, D.C.: U.S. Government Printing Office.

1980   Estimates of the population of the United States, by age, race, and sex: 1976 to 1979. Current Population Reports, Series P-25, No. 870. Washington, D.C.: U.S. Government Printing Office.

U.S. National Center for Health Statistics, Public Health Service

1957   *Vital Statistics of the United States 1955,* Vol. 1. Washington, D.C.: U.S. Government Printing Office.

1964   *Vital Statistics of the United States 1962,* Vol. 2. Washington, D.C.: U.S. Government Printing Office.

1969   *Vital Statistics of the United States 1967,* Vol. 1. Washington, D.C.: U.S. Government Printing Office.

1975   *Decennial Life Tables for 1969–71,* Vol. 1, No. 1: United States Life Tables: 1969–71. Washington, D.C.: U.S. Government Printing Office.

1978a   *Vital Statistics of the United States 1976,* Vol. 2, Section 5. Washington, D.C.: U.S. Government Printing Office.

1978b   *Vital Statistics of the United States 1975,* Vol. 1. Washington, D.C.: U.S. Government Printing Office.

1978c   *Vital Statistics of the United States 1975,* Vol. 2. Washington, D.C.: U.S. Government Printing Office.

1980a   *Vital Statistics of the United States 1978,* Vol. 2, Section 5: Life Tables. Washington, D.C.: U.S. Government Printing Office.

1980b   *Decennial Life Tables for 1969–71,* Vol. 1, No. 5: United States Life Tables by Causes of Death: 1969–71. Washington, D.C.: U.S. Government Printing Office.

Wolfenden, Hugh H.
    1954   *Population Statistics and Their Compilation,* revised edition. Chicago: University of Chicago Press.